This book would not be possible without the love and support of my late husband, Richard Rembert; and my three amazing children, Joe, Ricky and Reba.

Special acknowledgment to Dr. Angela Laverne Farr Griffin, who inspired me to share my story.

May this book inspire you to break your life's chains, and make lasting change.

CONTENTS

Foreword: A Letter to You, Dear Reader 1
Chapter 1: When Words Wouldn't Come 3
Chapter 2 Roots and Displacement 5
Chapter 3: The Question That Haunted Me 7
Chapter 4: Family Found And Lost 9
Chapter 5: Learning In Silence 11
Chapter 6: The Mystery Solved 13
Chapter 7: Understanding the Why 15
Chapter 8: A Father's Love 17
Chapter 9: The Mechanic's Heart 19
Chapter 10: Finding New Mothers 21
Chapter 11: Growing Up Too Fast 23
Chapter 12: The First Step to Independence 25
Chapter 13: Lessons from the Streets 27
Chapter 14: The Search for My Son 29
Chapter 15: Learning about Prejudice 32
Chapter 16: Finding My Way 34
Chapter 17: An Unlikely Guardian Angel 36
Chapter 18: Standing on My Own 38
Chapter 19: Building Something Real 40
Chapter 20: Finding Stability 42
Chapter 21: Opening My Heart 44
Chapter 22: New Beginnings 46

Chapter 23: Love and Family 48
Chapter 24: The Best Father Joe Ever Had 50
Chapter 25: Creating Our Home... 52
Chapter 26: Adventures and Challenges 55
Chapter 27: Building Wealth with Purpose... 57
Chapter 28: Success with Meaning 59
Chapter 29: Finding My Mission 61
Chapter 30: A House of Hope 63
Chapter 31: Community and Purpose 66
Chapter 32: Wisdom for the Next Generation.. 68
A Final Letter to You, Dear Reader 71
Epilogue: The Bridge of Healing.. 74
Reader Reflection Guide 78
Action Steps for Personal Growth.. 81
For Book Clubs and Group Discussions... 82
Resources for Further Help 83
Comprehensive Reader Reflection and Study Guide 84
Section 1: Personal Reflection Journey 85
Section 2: Book Club And Group Discussion Guide 88
Section 3: Therapeutic And Support Group Applications 93
Section 4: Educational Applications 95
Section 5: Action Steps And Resources... 97
Section 6: Reflection Prompts For Journaling.. 101

FOREWORD

A LETTER TO YOU, DEAR READER

"The same power that brought me from silence to voice, from abandonment to purpose, is available to you too. Your story isn't over—it's just beginning."
— Nellie Rembert

Pull up a chair, get comfortable, and let me tell you something important before we begin this journey together.

When I first put pen to paper to write my story, I never imagined it would become what you're holding in your hands today. This memoir began as scattered pieces of my life, written frantically on scraps of paper whenever a memory surfaced—a desperate attempt to make sense of the chaos within me.

My pastors, Dr. Angela Laverne Farr Griffin and her husband, saw something in me and told me, "You gotta write it. You cannot keep this to yourself. People need to know what you've gone through." So I made them a promise that I would write it all down.

But this isn't just my story—it's a story about finding hope in the darkest places, discovering that we're never truly alone, and learning that our greatest wounds can become our greatest strengths. Whether you believe in God or not, whether you've experienced trauma or lived a charmed life, there's something in these pages for you.

You see, from the time I was five years old, I had an imaginary friend who kept me company through the loneliest nights and the hardest days. I didn't know then that this friend—who started as conversations with two broken sticks I found while playing—was actually my lifeline to something greater than myself. Some of you will recognize this friend as Jesus. Others might call it resilience, hope, or the human spirit's refusal to be broken.

Whatever you call it, that presence taught me that we all have the power to break the chains that bind us and build bridges to a better future.

My story isn't always pretty. I'll take you through abandonment, poverty, teen pregnancy, and moments when I wanted to give up entirely. But I'll also show you how ordinary people can become extraordinary through love, how strangers can become family, and how broken things can be made beautiful again.

Since you've chosen to join me on this journey, you're stuck with me now. I'll go off on tangents, but you'll get used to it. Your job is to learn from my failures and successes, to participate with me in this shared conversation. Together, we'll navigate the depths of my story, shedding light on trauma that doesn't have to define us and discovering the hope that lives within us all.

Ready or not? Let's dive in, my dear friend.

With love and hope,
Nellie

CHAPTER 1

WHEN WORDS WOULDN'T COME

THE SILENCE THAT STARTED EVERYTHING

When I was nine years old, I couldn't talk. I mean, I could hear everyone speaking, and they expected me to respond, but the words just wouldn't come out. It was like there was a dam inside of me, blocking them from escaping. That silence wasn't just about words—it was depression so deep it felt like drowning while standing on dry land.

Imagine being a kid, sitting there, watching everyone around you, their mouths moving, their voices echoing in your head, and you're stuck in this prison of your own silence. It was devastating. Pure, unfiltered trauma that I had no words to name or explain.

I didn't know what I was doing half the time, but there was this fire inside me, a desperate need to eventually share my story. Even then, in that silence, something was stirring—a purpose I couldn't yet understand.

During those wordless days, I discovered something that would change my life forever. While playing outside, I came across a stick and broke it into two pieces. One piece became my imaginary friend, and the other became me. I started to develop a relationship with this friend, talking to him when no one else could hear me speak.

This friend became my role model, my source of inspiration, my guiding star in the darkest of nights. In the corners of my mind, I found a room that was endless, just like my desire to break free from whatever was holding me back.

Looking back now, I understand that my imaginary friend wasn't imaginary at all. He was preparing me for the days to come—those overwhelming moments of trauma and pain that would shape me into who I was meant to become. He was teaching me, even in my silence, that I was never truly alone.

The truth is, we all have moments when words fail us, when life feels too heavy to bear. But in those moments of deepest silence, if we listen carefully, we might just hear the voice that will guide us home.

REFLECTION QUESTIONS:

- ~ Have you ever experienced a time when you felt unable to express what was happening inside you?
- ~ What or who has served as a source of comfort during your most difficult moments?
- ~ How might silence sometimes be a form of protection or preparation?

CHAPTER 2

ROOTS AND DISPLACEMENT

WHERE I COME FROM

I was born in 1941, amidst a world in chaos. Life wasn't easy back then, and the darkness of those days seeped into every corner of my existence. I came into this world during a time when being Black meant facing limitations at every turn, when society had its chains wrapped tightly around us, suffocating our spirits and limiting our dreams.

Born in Buffalo, New York, I was soon whisked away to Alabama like some kind of unwanted baggage. They handed me over to a woman I called Mama, though there was nothing motherly about the arrangement. Every step of that journey felt like marching further into an abyss, feeling those chains of uncertainty tighten around my little body.

As a child, I never had a birthday celebration or Christmas with toys and a decorative tree. No one ever said "I love you" or offered a word of encouragement. These painful experiences brought moments of hate and blame toward the world. However, even then, I looked deep within and began repairing each bit and piece, step by step, living every day with the goal of becoming whole.

But in the face of those chains, I found strength through my relationship with my imaginary friend. He was my lifeline, my escape from the madness, always there in the corners of my mind where that endless room provided refuge from the harsh world outside.

Growing up in Alabama during the 1940s and 50s meant navigating a world where segregation was law and hope seemed like a luxury we couldn't afford. Yet something inside me refused to accept that this was all life had to offer. I refused to be just another cog in a machine designed to keep me small.

As I grew older, the fights for civil rights echoed through the air, reverberating within my very core. I felt lost, caught between the complacency of the old ways and the passion of the new. But my imaginary friend reminded me that there had to be more to life than what society dictated.

It wasn't easy, breaking those chains of darkness that bound me. The world pushed back, trying to keep me in my place. But I refused to let circumstances define me. I yearned for freedom, for the opportunity to forge my own path, to leave behind a legacy that mattered.

This chapter of my life taught me that our origins don't determine our destinations. We might not choose where we start, but we can choose where we're going.

REFLECTION QUESTIONS:

- How have the circumstances of your birth or early childhood shaped your perspective on life?
- What "chains" have you had to break free from in your own journey?
- Who or what has been your source of hope when the world seemed stacked against you?

CHAPTER 3

THE QUESTION THAT HAUNTED ME

WHO AM I?

Where do I even begin? My life started with chains of darkness wrapping themselves around me, and for the longest time, I didn't even know who I really was. Picture this: born in Buffalo, New York, then handed over to a woman called Mama in Alabama. But let me tell you, there was nothing motherly about her care.

Things seemed normal enough, I suppose. What did I know back then? I was just a kid trying to make sense of this confusing world. Mama was pretty, and her hair was always in place. Everyone loved Mama. And then, just when I thought I had found some sense of belonging, Mama died.

Her passing shattered the fragile illusion that she was my mother. I thought I was the only child because I was usually alone. I don't remember her saying she loved me—at least, not very often. I can't recall anyone really expressing love for me, though I do remember her smiles.

The doubt filled my mind constantly. Did I do something wrong? Was I not good enough for her? These chains of doubt wrapped themselves around my heart, and I couldn't shake them off. When they handed me over to someone else, I felt like a piece of trash being tossed aside.

They sat with me, trying to convince me that we were family. But how could I believe them when they had already lied to me? That betrayal stuck with me and shaped how I viewed relationships for years to come.

I remember exploring their old house, climbing trees, and hanging around outside. It never felt like "my" house. This new "family" didn't want to be close, so I grew even closer to my imaginary friend.

Those nights spent talking to my imaginary friend became my therapy. God was there with me in that old house, helping me climb emotional walls and cling to hope for something better. I was so lonely, and God—my imaginary friend—was the only one who understood. He listened when no one else would. He made me feel like I mattered, like I was important.

I was five years old but felt like nothing—nothing but a burden to be passed around. No one bothered to see me, to hear my thoughts, to cherish my existence. But my imaginary friend saw me, and that made all the difference.

They called me "Baby Nell," not because I was the youngest, but because I cried all the time. I cried because I felt like something was missing, and it was the truth. Each time it seemed I had gotten used to being around people, separation came again.

But through all of this confusion and pain, my imaginary friend was teaching me something valuable: that my worth wasn't determined by other people's actions or acceptance. I was valuable simply because I existed.

REFLECTION QUESTIONS:

- Have there been times in your life when you questioned your worth or identity?
- How do you define yourself when others seem to reject or overlook you?
- What helps you remember your inherent value when life feels overwhelming?

CHAPTER 4

FAMILY FOUND AND LOST

SISTER, SISTER

By the time I was thirteen, I learned the devastating truth that I had a family I never really knew existed. The pieces of our lives had been scattered like a jigsaw puzzle with missing pieces, and no one had bothered to explain the picture until years later.

We had been split up, torn apart like a band-aid barely holding us together. One sister went one way, another went elsewhere, and they took me to my chosen family. My sister was three years older than me, and they decided to send her to a different part of the country. When I later learned about this separation, it changed my life forever.

Do you have any idea what that's like? For a child to feel like they have no family, no friends, and that everything is their fault? Life became something entirely different than what I'd hoped for. Darkness clung to me like a leech, sucking the light out of everything. I'd sit alone, feeling like a broken toy that no one wanted.

Because of this trauma, I started wetting the bed. The smell was terrible, and I discovered a strange thing—I would change clothes at night and wake up the next morning to find the clothes were dry, the bed was dry, but that odor remained on my body daily.

There should have been somebody there to give me a bath, shampoo my hair, or just hug me. Anything to ease some of the pain and trauma.

But I refuse to hold onto bitterness about it now. Desperation became my driving force, a hunger to find someone who would truly accept me.

For reasons I didn't understand then, they took me away and left the others behind. It felt like a betrayal that deepened my confusion and fueled the fire of questions within me.

But I didn't give up. This fire burned inside me, refusing to be extinguished. Rainy days might have brought gloom over my spirit, but I never stopped searching for that silver lining. Maybe it was in those dark nights with my imaginary friend that I caught a glimpse of what it felt like to belong.

Despite all the trauma, pain, and loneliness, there were moments that made it all worthwhile. Moments when my stepmother Ida's embrace began to feel like home. Those moments gave me hope, reminding me that there was a world beyond those chains, beyond the darkness that threatened to consume me.

Later in my life, my siblings would play a pivotal role in my growth and development. The connection I once had with my biological family became a distant memory, but we still carried our father's distinctive features—tokens of our mixed heritage and reminders of our connection.

The separation from my siblings taught me something profound about family: it's not just about blood relations, but about the people who choose to love and support you. My imaginary friend was showing me that family could be found in unexpected places.

REFLECTION QUESTIONS:

- ∼ How has family separation or dysfunction affected your life?
- ∼ What does "family" mean to you beyond biological relationships?
- ∼ How do you find belonging when your original family structure is broken?

CHAPTER 5

LEARNING IN SILENCE

SCHOOL DAYS AND SILENT STRUGGLES

Growing up in the early 1950s, education was strictly regulated, and there was an issue with my birth records that prevented me from attending school initially. I don't remember much about those early years, but I remember that I didn't talk at all except to say yes or no. Instead of speaking, I would nod my head.

I constantly searched for answers—the truth that would ease my pain and trauma. But I never gave up. I took one day at a time, looking for peace in my life. Even when I felt unloved, I never wanted to take that pain out on others. My imaginary friend, God, helped me carry these heavy burdens.

I still didn't understand why I seemed to be different from other children. As time passed, I yearned for the freedom to just be a child, but the weight of responsibility and confusion hung over me. I dreamt of a different life while surrounded by the same shadows and darkness.

I was about nine to ten years old when I remember feeling desperate, struggling to learn rather than simply know facts. I didn't want any more pain and trauma. I spent many nights crying into wet pillows. In my heart, I spoke kind words and was gentle with my feelings, just like my son Joe would be later in life.

All I wanted was to be accepted so people would like me, not knowing that God heard my prayers all the time. My life began to feel fulfilled because I had God, my imaginary friend, as my constant companion.

What I didn't realize then was that my imaginary friend was preparing me for something greater. In those quiet moments of struggling to find my voice, he was teaching me that true communication comes from the heart, not just from words.

The education system couldn't accommodate my needs, but my imaginary friend was providing a different kind of education—one that would serve me for a lifetime. He was teaching me patience, resilience, and the power of quiet observation.

During this time, I discovered that learning doesn't always happen in a classroom. Sometimes the most valuable lessons come from sitting quietly and listening to that voice within that guides us toward truth and understanding.

My silence wasn't a disability—it was a different way of processing the world around me. While other children learned through conventional methods, I was developing a deeper understanding of human nature and emotional intelligence that would serve me throughout my life.

REFLECTION QUESTIONS:

- Have you ever felt different from others in a way that made learning or connecting difficult?
- What alternative forms of education or growth have shaped you outside traditional systems?
- How has quiet observation or reflection contributed to your understanding of the world?

CHAPTER 6

THE MYSTERY SOLVED

REDISCOVERY OF FAMILY

In the winter of 2016, down in Georgia, someone finally solved the mystery of our upbringing. At my sister Al's funeral, my cousin remembered seeing me and my siblings together in the southern part of the country where we were born. We had been separated so early that we had all become disconnected from each other.

That's when my bedwetting as a child finally made sense—it had begun because I was disconnected from my family structure. That trauma response was my little body's way of expressing the loss I couldn't put into words.

My sister and I thought we were discovering each other for the first time at the funeral, but my cousin revealed that we had actually been together with our father all along. My sister didn't believe our father had found us, partly because of his light skin color and blue eyes, which were so different from ours. With our mother being "jet black," we couldn't understand how we were all connected.

It was a heart-wrenching revelation to learn that there were two other siblings we'd never known about. The weight of this truth crushed us. Our father tried his best to mend our broken hearts by sharing as much as he could about our family history.

During this difficult period, I found solace in the one constant source of comfort I'd always had. I felt blessed to have had an imaginary friend early in life, only to realize that he wasn't imaginary at all—his real name was Jesus.

With the support of my brother-in-law and sister's husband, we embarked on a search for our mother. Her name was Pearl, and her beauty served as a bittersweet reminder of the pain we were about to uncover. How could a mother give away all of her children? This question haunted our journey.

We also discovered we had a brother who had passed away as an infant. Each new piece of information was like finding another piece of a puzzle that would never be complete, but at least we were beginning to see the full picture.

The discovery of our true family history was both devastating and healing. It explained so much about the abandonment issues, the constant feeling of not belonging, and the desperate need to create family wherever I found myself.

But most importantly, it confirmed what my imaginary friend had been telling me all along: I was never truly alone. Even when human family failed me, there was a greater family—a spiritual connection that could never be broken.

This revelation taught me that sometimes the truth takes decades to surface, but when it does, it brings both pain and incredible healing. Understanding our history doesn't erase the trauma, but it helps us make sense of our reactions and responses.

REFLECTION QUESTIONS:

- ~ Have there been family secrets or missing pieces in your own history that shaped your identity?
- ~ How do you process painful truths about your family or origins?
- ~ What role does spiritual family play when biological family is absent or dysfunctional?

CHAPTER 7

UNDERSTANDING THE WHY

WHY US?

Between the ages of ten and fifteen, attending school felt strange, and I'm not even sure I did consistently. I believe we were still living in Alabama before eventually moving to New York. The constant pull and push of different directions brought up the same anxiety and depression I'd been carrying.

During this time, I found myself in the company of an integrated family whose kindness offered a glimpse of acceptance and belonging. I sensed a connection to my father's side through their mixed heritage, but that bond disappeared almost as quickly as it had appeared.

My father, a master of disappearing acts, drifted in and out of my life, leaving behind unresolved questions and lingering pain. This pattern of abandonment by the men in my life would continue and deeply affect my ability to trust.

Growing up with my siblings and me being separated early in life made each of us feel alone. This is where the story of the five children I took in at age twenty-one begins. Their mother had died, and there I was—a newlywed—going to court to get custody of five children. I couldn't figure out why I'd be so determined to take on five children when I had just gotten married.

It was because of that disconnection that had been forced upon us three siblings at an early age. The trauma was consuming me. My mind was consumed by remembering the sadness, and my actions were driven by a desperate need to prevent other children from experiencing that same separation.

These people who raised me didn't beat me or rob me of anything material. That's not why I was depressed. I was depressed because my two siblings had been taken away from me. I realized that if I hadn't taken those five children when their mother died, something precious would have been taken from them too. That would have destroyed me and made them depressed as well.

As my father reconnected with me sporadically, my fears and uncertainties shaped me into a confused teenager. Fear has a way of consuming the best within us, burning away our potential and leaving room for darkness.

The separation from my siblings created a pattern in my life where I would go to extreme lengths to keep families together. It became both my greatest strength and my biggest vulnerability. I couldn't bear to see children separated from each other because I knew firsthand the lifelong impact of that trauma.

This experience taught me that our pain often becomes our purpose. The very thing that wounded us most deeply can become the driving force behind our greatest contributions to the world.

My imaginary friend was using my pain to develop my calling. He was showing me that my suffering wasn't meaningless—it was preparing me to be a lifeline for others who would face similar struggles.

REFLECTION QUESTIONS:

- ~ How has your deepest pain shaped your purpose or calling in life?
- ~ What patterns from your childhood do you find yourself repeating or deliberately breaking?
- ~ How might God or the universe be using your struggles to prepare you for future service?

CHAPTER 8

A FATHER'S LOVE

MY NEW FAMILY

In 1954, I went to live with my father, Larry. He was a compassionate individual who was always willing to lend a helping hand. He had a unique way of creating connections, often reaching out to anyone in need with a simple, "I'm Larry, let me help you."

Our father tried his best to mend our broken hearts, knowing that many sisters who had been separated were left with hate, division, deception, and bitterness. He kept our lines of communication open because he understood we needed him in our lives.

I distinctly recall his encouragement to always strive for the best. "Be your best because you are the best," he would tell us. These words became my guiding light, even though there were numerous unanswered questions and I often found myself shrouded in silence and depression.

My presence was silent, and I spoke through silence as well. I became known as "silent" during those times of turmoil and depression. However, my life took a positive turn when my dad married a remarkable woman named Ida.

Her presence brought hope, and I realized that life was indeed worth living. What nobody knew was that around this time, I had begun contemplating suicide. The pain felt unbearable, and I couldn't see a way forward.

My stepmother Ida suggested that I needed counseling, and she had connections at Huntington Hospital in Long Island, where she worked as the head nurse. I began therapy, and life started to take on new meaning.

She taught me how to transform hatred into love, how to navigate life's challenges with resilience, and how to replace anger with a smile. Most importantly, she emphasized the importance of forgiveness—not just forgiving others, but forgiving myself for thoughts and feelings that seemed too heavy for a child to carry.

What I realized from those therapy sessions was revolutionary: nothing was wrong with me. I had been left in the dark about so many things, given so little education about how to take care of myself emotionally and mentally. The silence, the withdrawal, the depression—these were normal responses to abnormal circumstances.

Discovering that I had multiple disabilities when I turned fifteen was both shocking and relieving. Multiple disabilities that I didn't even realize were disabilities—they were just part of me, silently affecting my confidence and sense of self.

The trauma I had experienced had affected my ability to think clearly and trust others. It whispered constantly, "Here we go again, another home to live in." But with my father's love and Ida's guidance, I began to understand that not every change meant another abandonment.

This was my first real experience of what healthy family looked like. My father's integrity and Ida's nurturing showed me that families could be built on love and choice, not just biology.

REFLECTION QUESTIONS:

- ∼ Who has served as a father or mother figure in your life when your biological parents couldn't fulfill that role?
- ∼ How has therapy or counseling helped you understand yourself better?
- ∼ What does healthy family look like to you, and how do you create it in your own life?

CHAPTER 9

THE MECHANIC'S HEART

MY FATHER'S CHARACTER

Let me paint you a picture of my father and the kind of man he was. My father had integrity and honesty that shone through in everything he did. He was a straight shooter, a man of his word who made it in the world not by manipulating or playing games, but by being true to himself and others.

He owned a car repair shop, and people trusted him completely. Customers would bring their vehicles in and leave the keys without a worry in the world because they knew he was a man of integrity who would do right by them. He didn't just earn money—he earned respect.

My father treated everyone with honesty and fairness, not just in business dealings but with kindness and understanding. He had this way of making you feel seen, heard, and valued. That, my friend, is worth more than all the money in the world.

Through his work as a mechanic for the Jewish community's transportation needs, he built connections and left a lasting impact on those he encountered. His dedication and service spoke volumes, and it became clear that his influence transcended his immediate circle.

I remember the diesel truck company he worked with and the school buses he repaired. I can still recall the distinct memory of those Jewish school buses where only Jewish children rode. It was a glimpse into a culture and community I had never experienced before, and my father served as a bridge between worlds.

He repaired their vehicles with the same care and attention he gave to everyone else's, regardless of race or religion. In a time when segregation was the norm, my father's workshop became a place where character mattered more than color.

Watching my father work taught me valuable lessons about integrity in business and life. He showed me that you can succeed without stepping on others, that honest work has dignity, and that respect is earned through consistent character, not inherited through status.

My father wasn't just successful in business—he was an example of how to live with honor. He demonstrated that you can make it in this world not by tearing others down, but by lifting them up and being true to yourself and those around you.

This legacy of honesty, integrity, and respect became the foundation I would build my own life upon. Years later, when I became successful in real estate and business, I remembered my father's example and strove to conduct myself with the same character he had shown me.

REFLECTION QUESTIONS:

- Who has modeled integrity and honest work in your life?
- How do you balance success with maintaining your values and character?
- What kind of legacy do you want to leave through your work and relationships?

CHAPTER 10

FINDING NEW MOTHERS

LEARNING LIFE'S LESSONS

Saturdays became special days when my father would take me along as he worked. Through his connections in the Jewish community, I learned about different traditions and beliefs. There were various groups—Jews for Jesus, traditional Jewish people, and Orthodox Brooklyn-based Jews. It was like navigating through a maze of different customs and beliefs.

In the summer of 1957, I received a job as a mother's helper with Mrs. LaGrange. Her husband worked for American Airlines, and she was a teacher in Douglaston, Queens. Every Saturday, I would spend time with their children—Jane and George LaGrange—playing in the yard, babysitting, and just being present.

Mrs. LaGrange became a guiding voice who provided wisdom and insight. She held a belief that practicing something at least five times could lead to mastery. "You'll receive it in your doing," she would say, emphasizing the importance of repetition and persistence. This simple yet profound lesson became a cornerstone of my approach to learning and life.

I adopted Mrs. LaGrange's philosophy in my interactions with children and those around me throughout my life. The idea that repeating something five times could lead to understanding and mastery became a guiding principle that I would later use in parenting and teaching others.

Now, let me tell you something important about those times: if your skin was dark like mine, many jobs were simply not available to people of color. But I got that position because my father worked as a mechanic for Temple Emanuel in Great Neck. It was through his connection and reputation that I was able to secure that summer job.

Life has a way of weaving together strange threads, doesn't it? Here I was, a girl with limited formal education, battling invisible disabilities, yet finding opportunities through the relationships my father had built through his honest work.

Mrs. LaGrange also taught me practical life skills that my own upbringing had missed. She showed me how to create a beautiful home environment, how to interact with children in nurturing ways, and how dedication to small details could create something beautiful.

Even in those times when mothers, especially mothers of color, were often confined to their homes with limited opportunities, Mrs. LaGrange showed me a different model of womanhood—one that combined education, grace, and purposeful work.

These experiences were shaping me for a future I couldn't yet imagine. My imaginary friend was putting people in my path who would teach me skills I would need later—not just for survival, but for thriving and helping others do the same.

REFLECTION QUESTIONS:

- Who has served as an unexpected teacher or mentor in your life?
- What simple principles or philosophies have guided your approach to learning and growth?
- How have you seen God or the universe provide opportunities through relationships?

CHAPTER 11

GROWING UP TOO FAST

ME AND MY JOE

During the same time I was working as a mother's helper, I met Joe's father through my stepmother Ida's nephew, Johnny Bolden. He introduced Joe's father to my dad when he needed car repairs. My father's customers were mainly white because there were only a few Black folks in our area at that time.

I need to be honest about what happened next because the truth, even when it's difficult, is what sets us free. Everyone said Joe's father took advantage of me, but the truth is more complicated. I was fifteen, desperate for love and attention that I wasn't getting from my own father. When an older man paid attention to me, I responded in ways I didn't fully understand.

I seduced him without even knowing what I was doing, reaching out for love, for care, for someone to see me. And he paid attention. I kept pursuing this attention, not realizing that sexuality was part of this destructive dance I was doing.

When I finally faced the truth about my role in what happened, it tore me apart. Standing up and telling the truth was incredibly hard because if they had taken him to court, he could have been arrested. But I had to acknowledge my part in what occurred.

This pattern isn't new. From way back in slavery times, young girls have been reaching out to older men, desperate for attention and affection they weren't getting from their fathers. It's a cycle that continues today.

These young girls don't understand that men often think with their bodies, not their hearts. They don't see the pain and hurt in these girls—they just see opportunity. It's devastating, but it's the truth.

I became pregnant at fifteen while still working with Mrs. LaGrange. Joe was born in early September, and my summer job had finished. My stepmother Ida sensed something was different and took me to the doctor. That's when I learned I was carrying a child, all alone, with nobody knowing my truth.

A check for $91.10 used to come in the mail for Joe. I had no idea what it was for initially, but it was child support from Joe's father, arranged legally though I wasn't aware of the details at the time.

At eighteen, when most young adults were finding regular employment, I found myself blocked from getting jobs because my father, trying to help, had given me three different social security numbers for different schools. The paperwork couldn't keep up, and it created a mess that took years to sort out.

But through all of this confusion and struggle, Mrs. LaGrange's words rang in my ears: "Don't be like your mother. Do whatever you have to do to get your son back and keep him with you."

During those tough times, I clung to my son Joe and held onto Mrs. LaGrange's support. She offered us an open door whenever we needed housing, and that stability was something I knew I could depend on.

REFLECTION QUESTIONS:

- ~ How do we take responsibility for our choices while also acknowledging when we've been vulnerable or exploited?
- ~ What role does desperation for love and attention play in the decisions we make?
- ~ How can we break generational cycles of dysfunction and create healthier patterns?

CHAPTER 12

THE FIRST STEP TO INDEPENDENCE

STEPPING OUT

In the summer of 1959, I learned some shocking news that would change everything. My father had been having an affair with a woman named Juanita who lived in Hempstead. She had her own children, and I could see he was spending more time at her house than just fixing her car.

One night, my stepmother Ida and my father were arguing in the kitchen, and he said something inappropriate to her. I don't remember the exact words, but they hurt to hear after everything she had done for him and for us. I was standing by the broom closet, and I just started hitting him. I was so angry at him for speaking to her that way when she had been nothing but good to us.

Ida left money on the table for me and told me to stay with her sister Lula for the night. I later found out that this money came from the child support checks Joe's father had been sending—$91.10 that I never knew I was receiving because no one had explained anything to me.

Lula had many children and no husband. She was beautiful with straight hair and stunning blue eyes, just like my father. But there was a catch to staying with her: I had to give her all the money my stepmother had left for me. I needed shelter for Joe and me, so I gave her everything.

Then the lights went out in our house in Green Lawn, and my father wasn't there to fix them. It was just me and Joe in the darkness. When I called Ida for help, she arranged for us to stay with Lula temporarily.

But Lula got jealous of her boyfriend Alfonso, accusing me of trying to steal him when I had no interest in him whatsoever. Instead of dealing with her own insecurities, she took it out on me and told me to get out.

Meanwhile, my father had left to find Ida, who had gone to Topeka, Kansas, to stay with her brother Jeff. She couldn't take his infidelity anymore. After everything she had done—marrying him, accepting me and my son, helping us all heal—he had betrayed her trust.

So there I was, once again alone with my son. I asked Lula for half my money back, which she gave me wrapped in paper rather than in an envelope. With that small amount, Joe and I made our way to Huntington Station and the Long Island Railroad.

This was my first real step toward independence, though it certainly didn't feel empowering at the time. It felt terrifying and lonely. But my imaginary friend was with us on that train, and I knew somehow that we would survive this too.

Looking back, I can see that this crisis forced me to start building the independence and resilience I would need for the journey ahead. Sometimes we have to lose everything before we can discover what we're truly capable of building.

REFLECTION QUESTIONS:

- Have there been times when crisis forced you toward independence before you felt ready?
- How do you find strength when the people you depend on let you down?
- What role does faith or hope play when you're facing uncertainty with children depending on you?

CHAPTER 13

LESSONS FROM THE STREETS

HELEN AND JUANITA

Later that year, when I met Helen and Juanita, Joe and I were essentially homeless, couch-surfing in the living rooms of my father's friends. Helen and Juanita were always well-dressed, always seemed to have money in their pockets. It would have been easy to turn jealous, but instead, I mustered up the courage to ask them where they worked and if they had any openings.

They giggled and exchanged glances. One of them said, "You're pretty." I thanked them and tried again: "Where do you work?" Then Juanita chimed in, "You've got a nice body." I had no clue why they were fixating on my looks and body until later when I learned the truth—they were call girls.

After giving birth to Joe, I wasn't allowed to continue working as a mother's helper because my job had been to take care of other children. With no education and nowhere to stay, I agreed to give this new line of work a try.

My first "client" was a white man. We met at the St. James Hotel where Helen and Juanita had rooms. When he walked in and stripped bare, I froze. I had never seen a naked man, especially not a white one. Every smile he gave made me sick inside. When I couldn't perform as expected, he quickly dressed, left money on the table, and left.

I tried two more times with different men, but the same thing happened each time. I couldn't go through with it. My 15-year-old experience with intimacy haunted me, and I realized this wasn't something I could do.

Three clients later, I never had to degrade myself, and they still left me money. Maybe they feared their wives finding out if they didn't pay, or maybe they respected my obvious discomfort. I handed half the money to Helen as agreed, but I knew this wasn't my path.

I decided that the next time I would be intimate with a man, he would be my husband. And I meant it. My imaginary friend was looking after me even then, protecting me from a path that would have destroyed my spirit.

This experience taught me several important things: First, desperation can lead us to consider choices that go against our deepest values. Second, sometimes God protects us even when we're making questionable decisions. And third, our traumatic experiences, while painful, can sometimes serve as protective mechanisms that keep us from even greater harm.

I also learned that there are people in this world who will try to exploit young women who are vulnerable and desperate. But there are also moments when grace intervenes, when something greater than ourselves steps in to redirect our path.

REFLECTION QUESTIONS:

- ∽ Have there been times when desperation led you to consider choices that conflicted with your values?
- ∽ How have you seen protection or intervention in your life when you were vulnerable?
- ∽ What experiences have taught you to set and maintain boundaries, even in difficult circumstances?

CHAPTER 14

THE SEARCH FOR MY SON

KIDNAPPED

Mrs. LaGrange confronted me about why I kept sending Joe away. I told her I needed work, couldn't get other jobs because of my social security number problems, and couldn't even go to school. She looked at me with judgment and said, "You're going to end up just like your mother, with your child scattered all over the place."

Her words crushed my heart because I knew that feeling of abandonment, and I never wanted anyone to feel that way, especially not my Joe. But I didn't have a stable place for him to stay.

Then she hit me with words that cut deep: "Wherever you sleep, that's where he sleeps. He doesn't care about anything else—he just needs to be with you." She was right. If you truly love your child, you do whatever it takes to keep them with you.

I decided to go back to Alabama to Maxwell Air Force Base to get my son from my sister. But when I arrived, she told me Joe's father had taken him. She said he went with his father willingly, and she thought I knew about it.

I collapsed on the floor and cried. In my mind, he had kidnapped my child. Why would he take Joe away from my sister in Alabama? It felt like every part of my life was being torn apart.

I went to the bus station and told my story to the bus driver. He put me in the seat behind him and said, "I'll make sure you get to Ohio, but then you're going to have to take care of yourself because I don't know the whole story."

Each driver I encountered heard my story and helped me continue my journey. I ended up taking three different buses. Imagine this: a young Black girl in 1959, traveling across the country frantically searching for her son.

When I reached the address I had, there were no homes—only businesses. I didn't have a home address for Joe's father, so I started going door to door in residential areas, asking everyone I saw about a little boy. I didn't even have a picture to show people.

People were different back then—more loving, friendly, and caring. I made my way down Livingston Avenue, going from door to door on both sides of the street. I should have asked about Joe and his grandmother Rebecca instead of just his father, because people knew the woman Joe was staying with.

When I started asking about Rebecca, my luck changed. They said they saw a little boy with her every day. On the third day of my search, while sitting on someone's steps talking to my imaginary friend Jesus, God worked a miracle.

I didn't know what Rebecca looked like, and people were hesitant to trust me. But somehow, God brought us together. When I told her my story, she said, "Are you Baby Nell?" Everyone had called me that growing up because I cried all the time.

When I said yes and told her I was Joe's mother, she hugged me. She said, "I knew one day you were coming." Those words put hope back in my soul.

And I did it—I got my son back. Joe had been living with his grandmother, not his father. She had been taking care of Joe because she knew his father was going to die, though I didn't know this at the time.

REFLECTION QUESTIONS:

- How far would you go to protect or reclaim what matters most to you?
- Have you experienced times when strangers showed unexpected kindness during your darkest moments?
- What role does persistence play when you're fighting for your family?

CHAPTER 15

LEARNING ABOUT PREJUDICE

IN BLACK AND WHITE

I came back to New York on the bus with Joe, and Mrs. LaGrange gave me my job back. My son slept at the foot of the bed while I slept at the top in her house. Mrs. LaGrange's children, George and Jane, became like family to Joe. Despite being just three years old, Joe remembered them, and they loved each other like brothers and sisters. They didn't see color—none of them did.

Mr. LaGrange was an airline pilot who worked for American Airlines. He always had that crisp white shirt with epaulets on the shoulders and his pilot's cap. Every time he came home, he would put the cap on Joe's head first, then on Jane's, and finally on his own son's head. It was such an open, loving gesture.

I can't remember a single incident where Blacks and whites were separated in my immediate environment in New York. Maybe it's because I didn't want to see it, or maybe nobody showed it to me directly. The only incident I witnessed happened when the neighbor's son had a birthday party.

Joe wasn't invited. They invited Jane and her brother, but not Joe. They didn't even bother to put his name on the invitation.

I was coming up from the basement when I heard Mrs. LaGrange on the phone, explaining how Joe wasn't invited. She told them he wasn't available, so why bother including his name? I thought to myself, "Are you kidding me? You should have called and let me know that Joe was invited too!"

But then Mrs. LaGrange said something that stuck with me: "I don't want my children to ever feel like they can go to a birthday party and leave their friend Joe here alone." That hit me hard. She was explaining prejudice in a way that made sense to me.

That incident made me realize that Mrs. LaGrange was teaching her children something valuable about loyalty and inclusion. She wouldn't let them participate in exclusion, even when it was socially acceptable to do so.

It also taught me that there are people who will stand up against prejudice not just with words, but with actions. Mrs. LaGrange could have just sent her children to the party and explained it away, but instead she used it as a teaching moment about doing what's right.

This experience showed me that fighting prejudice isn't always about big dramatic gestures. Sometimes it's about the small daily decisions to include rather than exclude, to stand with people rather than abandon them when it's inconvenient.

Mrs. LaGrange was modeling for her children—and for me—what it looks like to choose relationship over social acceptance, love over convenience.

REFLECTION QUESTIONS:

- When have you witnessed someone taking a stand against exclusion or prejudice?
- How do you teach children (or learn yourself) to choose inclusion over social acceptance?
- What small daily decisions can we make to fight prejudice and build bridges between communities?

CHAPTER 16

FINDING MY WAY

A LONG WAY FROM HOME

By the time I turned twenty, I needed to make my own way. Opportunities were few for an uneducated Black girl in 1960s New York. Joe and I went to Port Jefferson Station, just a stone's throw from where we'd been staying. We waited at the station until morning for the train that left at three or four o'clock.

We hopped on the train coming from Huntington, but I didn't have a ticket. I had never experienced buying a ticket before and didn't understand how it worked. I was the only one without a ticket on that train, and the conductor kept passing me by, seeing me there with my little boy.

When everyone got off at Jamaica Station, I stayed put because I knew the train would go back. I had to catch another one to get to Manhattan. The conductor saw us ride those trains multiple times. He even gave Joe a blanket and his jacket to keep him warm.

He finally said, "You have to get off here." He didn't mention anything about finding places to stay, but he hinted that I would find people who could help me. It took me a while to figure out he meant I would find Black people I could connect with, since all the people on the train were white.

I got off at Broadway Junction, heading toward Brooklyn, hoping to meet someone who could help us. That's when I went to the park and met Bob. It was in that part of Brooklyn that my journey took another important turn.

Bob saw me in that rundown park where he used to go after working nights. He slept on a pallet, exhausted but determined to stay fit. Joe and I spent the whole day there, and we had to find some food.

I went to the A&P on Merrill Avenue, where they had a section for discounted food. I grabbed whatever I could, not caring about the quality. But then something amazing happened—a man saw me struggling and told me to take whatever I needed. It was always like that—people, complete strangers, reaching out to help me when I needed it most.

That's when I poured my heart out to Bob. I told him about my struggles, about how I wasn't always fighting to survive like this. Bob told me something that stuck with me—he said he admired me. Someone, in the midst of their own hardships, found strength and inspiration in my story.

Then he asked the question that had been haunting me: "Where are you going to stay?" I didn't have an answer. But Bob showed me a way. He lived on 94 Ryson Street in Brooklyn, between Flesh and Merrill Avenue.

There was a catch—no children were allowed in his building. My heart ached at the thought of leaving Joe behind, but Bob helped me figure out a way to keep us together.

REFLECTION QUESTIONS:

- ~ Have there been times when you've had to rely on the kindness of strangers?
- ~ How do you maintain hope and dignity when you have very limited options?
- ~ What does it mean to find family and home in unexpected places?

CHAPTER 17

AN UNLIKELY GUARDIAN ANGEL

WHAT ABOUT BOB

Bob became like a big brother, a friend, and a protector all rolled into one. During the day, he'd take Joe out to the park, keeping him occupied while I hustled to make ends meet. Bob fell in love with me, but I didn't realize it until much later. I needed him, and I looked at him as someone who cared, someone I could rely on.

Bob was a handsome man with a good heart. I didn't have any money—I was flat broke and desperate. When Bob came home from work one day, I decided it was time for me to get a job. That's when Bob told me about Academy on Warren Street in Brooklyn.

I lied to the guy at the Academy because I didn't want him to know I was completely broke. I told him I worked for Larry's garage—my dad's business. I practiced answering the phone: "Good morning, Larry's garage! Can I help you?" I kept saying it over and over, trying to act like I knew what I was doing.

Somehow, my little fib worked. They sent me out on a job, and the next day they said they were hiring me from the academy. I got the job on the spot—no experience required. I called it the work of God, my imaginary friend who had been with me all along.

The first day I stepped foot into that place in Maspeth, Queens, I had to practice my greeting. "Good morning, Coney's!" I had to say it five times at the academy. That job was my door opening to opportunity, to a chance at a better life.

There was this heavy-set lady at the academy who wasn't friendly at all. She moved me to the front desk and said I needed to practice. She caught me throwing papers in the garbage when I made mistakes because I didn't want her to see my errors.

Every day I was taking notes and making mistakes. The next day, on my way back to work, taking the Flushing Avenue bus to Maspeth Queens, I discovered I didn't have enough money. The fare had gone up from 10 cents to 15 cents, but I only had 10 cents.

The bus driver saw my situation. He put his hand over the slot and said, "You paid." I was confused at first, but I figured out what he was saying: "Come on in."

It was like God was still protecting me, still watching over me. I don't know why that man covered the slot, but it saved me. I made it to work, even though my money didn't last long.

Bob lived upstairs on the second floor while Joe and I were on the ground level. The couple who ran the place seemed to be connected to a church, and they broke their own rules by letting me in with Joe.

Children weren't allowed because they worried about crying and noise, but Joe was always humble and quiet. When we'd come home, he'd say things like "Happy Monday," and their faces would light up. It's always nice to hear a child being polite.

Bob wanted more from our relationship, but I wasn't ready for that. I didn't understand how to give my body away just to keep a man around, like some people suggested I should.

REFLECTION QUESTIONS:

~ Who has served as an unexpected guardian angel in your life?
~ How do you navigate relationships when you need help but aren't ready for certain expectations?
~ What small acts of kindness from strangers have made a big difference in your journey?

CHAPTER 18

STANDING ON MY OWN

ON MY OWN

I talked to Matthew, the brother of the company owner, about needing extra hours to make more money. He said I could come in half an hour early in the morning and stay half an hour late, giving me one extra hour of pay. It wasn't the full hour I wanted, but I had to make it work.

I worked harder than anyone else, doing everything I could to show them I was somebody worth keeping. I cleaned, organized, and went above and beyond. The owner's brother said it wasn't fair for me to do all that extra work, but the owner gave me a raise anyway.

Then he said I could come in on Saturdays for four extra hours. The bus driver kept covering the fare slot with his hand, letting me ride for free that whole week when I couldn't afford the increased fare. God's favor was evident, telling me not to stop, not to quit.

Every step of the way, God was guiding me because He knew I could have fallen into all sorts of traps if He hadn't been available for me. While all this was happening, Joe didn't have to pay anything, and I saved my money.

After I saved enough, I decided to move out and get my own apartment. When my father and Ida came back to Huntington from Kansas, I told them everything that had happened, including how Lula had accused me of trying to have an affair with her boyfriend. It was all because of her own insecurities and distorted thinking.

I was finally able to go back and forth to Huntington with Joe. We could get potatoes from a nearby field, and that's mostly what we had—potatoes, trying to make do with what little we had. Joe was humble about it, eating potatoes day in and day out without complaining.

No one knew what I was going through at night. I remember there weren't individual ketchup packets back then, and every day I'd try to sneak some extra ketchup. One guy saw me struggling and put some ketchup in a bottle for me. That meant the world—it's amazing how something as small as free ketchup can brighten your day.

Here we were in our own place in Brooklyn, living off a 10-pound bag of potatoes and bottles of ketchup. Every day, that's what we had. It was what we could afford, and it kept us going.

When I told Bob that I couldn't be with him the way he wanted, he respected that and continued to help me out. Going back to Huntington on weekends was a different world—Joe would play outside, and my stepmother would cook big meals for us.

But when it was time to head back to Brooklyn, Joe didn't want to go. It always broke my heart to leave him there, hearing him say, "See you later, Nell."

Eventually, I told my father what had really happened—that I was innocent of what Lula had accused me of. My parents kept Joe in Huntington while I stayed on Ryson Street, saving every penny I had.

REFLECTION QUESTIONS:

- ~ How do you maintain dignity and hope when living with very basic necessities?
- ~ What role does hard work play in building self-respect and creating opportunities?
- ~ How do you handle relationships when your needs and someone else's expectations don't align?

CHAPTER 19

BUILDING SOMETHING REAL

A PLACE TO CALL HOME

Ever Ready Furniture store claimed to have everything ready to furnish your entire home, but they were anything but ready to help someone like me. It's this massive place on Broadway in Brooklyn. When I walked in and asked about credit, the response was predictable.

"We do credit, but..." And there's always a "but," isn't there? He told me I didn't have enough working history. He said those exact words like a slap in the face: "You haven't been working long enough. Can't give you credit for furniture like that."

So I asked him where I was supposed to get credit from then. His answer? "When you work, you pay a down payment. If you pay for half of it, then maybe we'll give you credit."

But here's the thing—I actually did it. Every Friday when I got paid from Coney's company, I handed over money to that guy. It took me three, maybe four weeks, but I gave him the down payment for three whole rooms: kitchen, dinette, living room, and bedroom sets.

But now I needed money for an apartment to put the furniture in. It was Sunday, and snow was about to hit. I walked around on Ryson Street like someone possessed, checking every "apartment for rent" sign I could find.

Of course, they all wanted references, which I didn't have. I had no idea how much of a struggle this would be. I ended up completely defeated, hands freezing, feet numb, sitting on the steps at 438 Schanck Avenue in East New York.

I had given up on everything, sitting there covered in snow. I called out to my imaginary friend, asking why I had to suffer so much, just pouring my heart out to the heavens.

Then the landlord showed up. He saw me sitting there on those freezing steps covered in snow. He had to clear it off for his two-bedroom apartment. When I mentioned I was looking for a two-bedroom too, he said there was no light in the place—just a lamp in the hallway.

He said I could come back another day, but I couldn't take time off from my new job. It was freezing, and I was trying to keep my hands warm. I had my money stashed in my pocket, probably around $125.

I gave him the money right there. He said I needed a month's security and a month's rent, but he'd let me slide with just the rent. $125 for a place to stay in this crazy city.

When I came back to the apartment on Ryson Street, Bob asked me where my receipt was. What receipt? I didn't even know I was supposed to get one. Back in those days, your word was your bond. If you were honest, you didn't think about getting receipts.

Bob acted like I was some fool for not having one, suggesting the guy might have taken advantage of me. But he didn't take advantage of me. I may have been young and inexperienced, but I wasn't stupid.

The furniture store was holding my money, and I didn't even have the apartment yet. But I figured it out because I always do. It was just another obstacle to overcome on this journey of mine.

REFLECTION QUESTIONS:

- How do you persevere when systems seem designed to keep you out?
- What does it mean to build something from nothing with limited resources?
- How do you maintain hope when facing seemingly impossible challenges?

CHAPTER 20

FINDING STABILITY

IN BETWEENNESS

In the beginning of December 1963, my parents finally came to see the apartment in Brooklyn. I was proud of how it looked by then. My stepmother admired the way I hung the curtains and showed me how to create beautiful tiebacks for them. She taught me to open them during the day and close them at night, which really brought the living room together.

I had two end tables and two lamps—simple things, but they meant the world to me. These small touches made our place feel cozy and welcoming.

When I finally told my dad about everything, about how things had gotten better, my stepmother cried. She said she felt punished for leaving my dad during his affair, but she had left me money—more than what an average person would have done. From then on, she started helping me out, buying things for the apartment and for Joe.

My stepmother Ida was kind and loving in everything she did. She took me to Sears and bought me sheets, towels, and all sorts of things to help me out. But no matter how put together my apartment was, they still wouldn't let me have Joe full-time. They said I wasn't fit to be a mother and had nobody to watch him.

Everything was falling apart, but I had to make do. I wanted my son back. Mrs. LaGrange's words rang in my ears like a broken record: "Don't be like your mother. Do whatever you have to do to get your son back."

I used my clothes as bedding, sleeping on my winter clothes because it was spring and I didn't need them for warmth. I had to dress up every single day, no matter what. I wanted to look sharp like those white girls I saw who wore gloves that matched their outfits—pink gloves with a pink suit, yellow gloves with a yellow suit.

So I bought gloves to match my clothes. I wanted to fit in, to look professional. I went to work sharp every day, catching the bus at the corner of Myrtle Avenue and Broadway, heading to Coney's. Not a single person knew that I had been sleeping on the floor at 438 Schanck Avenue.

I found a couple who lived near a school and asked if they would watch Joe before and after school. I told them I'd pay, but they didn't want to hear any such thing. God provided a solution to my babysitting problem. With that taken care of and a decent place to live, my parents finally decided to let Joe live with me. He was five years old by this time.

I still wasn't the best chef, but Joe forgave me for it, and we got along just fine. Life taught me never to throw away food. We never waste food. Your past is your present and your future, and we've got to remember that and appreciate what we have.

REFLECTION QUESTIONS:

- How do you create beauty and dignity in challenging circumstances?
- What does it mean to dress for the life you want, not just the life you have?
- How do you build support systems when traditional family structures aren't available?

CHAPTER 21

OPENING MY HEART

CHARLETTE

In the winter of 1963, I hadn't had my furniture more than a month when I let Charlette move in with us. He was standing outside on Sutter Avenue, needing a place to stay. I had gotten bunk beds so Joe could have a proper bed, and there was an extra bed available.

I found out Charlette was gay when my neighbor, a so-called churchgoer, decided to stick her nose where it didn't belong. She had the audacity to tell me I had no right to have a gay man living in the same house as my son. She planted doubt in my head, making me worry about what might happen at night.

I became defensive. I couldn't stand the thought of someone discriminating against Charlette just because of who he was. Charlette was a joy to have around the house—he'd cook, clean, and even play with Joe when he was home.

I didn't tell my parents about Charlette's sexual orientation because I hadn't even known he was gay initially. I had never knowingly met a gay person before. My neighbor called him a horrible name and degraded me, telling me I should be ashamed for having my son around someone like that.

To this day, I can't remember her name because I don't pay attention to negativity. She also had the nerve to criticize me for "leaving my son to sleep on the porch." Let me give you some context: Little Joe had gotten out of school early and had nowhere to go. Nobody bothered to check the note in his backpack, so he figured out the bus routes and made his way home.

He walked all the way from Bedford-Stuyvesant to East New York, exhausted at just five years old. He sat on that porch and fell asleep. What did that "loving" neighbor do? She walked right past him without checking if he was okay.

But Charlette came home and rescued my baby. He took Joe inside and gave him a warm, safe place to rest. I was sick when I found out what had happened. Who was she to judge me as a mother when she couldn't even show basic decency to a child in need?

After that incident, I was in a dark place. Her words triggered all those insecurities I had about being a good mother. I was hearing Mrs. LaGrange's voice in my head, reminding me that I had to fight against my past and not repeat the same mistakes.

The next morning, I couldn't bring myself to take Joe to school or go to work. I just couldn't handle it. Ms. Alfred saw what was happening and offered to keep Joe during the week to ease his early morning travels so I could go to work without all the stress.

This experience taught me that we're all sinners, every single one of us. We all fall short. So who is anyone to point fingers at others? Rather than judging and criticizing, maybe we should focus on having more compassion and understanding.

REFLECTION QUESTIONS:

- How do you respond to judgment and criticism from others, especially when it involves people you care about?
- What does it mean to show love and acceptance to people who are different from you?
- How do you protect your peace while still standing up for what's right?

CHAPTER 22

NEW BEGINNINGS

ROSE

I don't know where she came from, but in January 1964, I met Rose. We crossed paths at the corner of Schanck and Sutter, and it didn't take long for us to strike up a conversation. Rose mentioned she was looking for a room, and while I didn't have a room to offer, I did have a bed we could share.

It was the four of us—Joe, Rose, me, and Charlette. We kept this arrangement hidden from Joe during the week since he was staying with Mr. and Mrs. Alfred for school.

Rose informed me that her brother Ray needed a place to stay, so we made room for him on the couch. All of us contributed to the rent in this communal arrangement.

One day, Rose's boyfriend George came by with a few friends and suggested we could make money by hosting card games at our place. Inspired by their idea, we decided to hold games on Friday and Saturday nights. George helped set things up, and one of his friends, Richard, acted as security.

We realized we could increase profits by selling food and liquor. Rose took charge of the cooking while I handled serving and entertaining. I had a natural knack for entertaining, perhaps influenced by my mother, who had been a dancer.

Thanks to the money from the card games and sales, none of us had to worry about rent. Joe stayed with the Alfreds during weekdays for school, and I would take him to my parents' house on weekends. He had no idea about the people living in our home or the activities we hosted.

Our arrangement lasted through the summer and into the fall, and during that time, we all grew incredibly close. It was a period of transformation for me as I slowly emerged from my shell.

One night after visiting a club in Brooklyn, I came back with Rose and Richard. Richard knocked on my door, wanting to come in, but I told him to sleep on the couch. I couldn't let him in, not with Rose around, and definitely not because I wasn't ready to get involved with any man.

But I opened up to Richard, telling him everything about myself. He shared his painful past too—growing up feeling lonely, depressed, and full of trauma. Our shared experiences of abandonment brought us close together and made us fall in love.

I don't think it was ever really romantic love at first, but a familiarity with pain. He became my therapist and I became his. That night, we grew closer, and I told him that any man who was with me would have to be my husband. He took me seriously.

We all earned our share of money and contributed to household expenses. As time went on, everyone saved up their earnings, and slowly but surely, each of us found separate places to live.

REFLECTION QUESTIONS:

- How do you create family and community with people who aren't related to you?
- What role does shared struggle play in forming deep relationships?
- How do you know when someone understands your pain and can help you heal?

CHAPTER 23

LOVE AND FAMILY

WE ARE FAMILY

It wasn't long after I turned twenty-three that Richard asked me to marry him. The day he proposed, they measured my fingers for a ring. I thought, "This is it. I'm finally going to get that ring." But it didn't happen that day, even though he did officially propose.

I couldn't wait to tell my stepmother. After they measured the ring size, I called her, bursting with excitement. But she was cautious. She said, "Let's think this through. If he acts strange, let your instincts guide you. We need to know if he's telling the truth."

Richard wanted to get married right away. He said he had been searching for someone like me for years and didn't want to let me go. He had been engaged once before, but they called it off before he went into the military. When he found me, he wanted to make me his wife immediately.

So we got married on October 29th, 1964. My stepmother secured my wedding dress and insisted I wear blue because I already had a child—that was just how things were done back then.

But it wasn't just the wedding that brought my life together—it was family. My dad, Ida, and my sister were there for me. Family is everything when you've spent so much of your life feeling alone.

We had the wedding right there at 438 Schanck Avenue. My husband Richard was a gentleman who didn't pressure me sexually until I was ready. But he wanted to start a family much more than I did, so I went along with it.

That was our foundation—supporting each other and acknowledging each other's trauma. We made sure we thought about how our actions would impact one another, and that became the cornerstone of our union.

Ida gave me crucial advice: "Before you judge others, think about the damage you're causing." She helped me understand that I needed to continue with my counselor to get through this marriage successfully. I followed her advice, and it worked.

On weekends, there were no more parties. Instead, Richard would cash his entire paycheck and bring it home, saying, "You used to manage the apartment before; manage it now however you want." He trusted me with our finances, and we had a good life starting off.

Richard started feeling uncomfortable with the landlord coming to collect rent from an apartment that was only in my name. He wanted us to have a different apartment with both our names on the lease, which made sense.

The foundation of our marriage was built on mutual respect, shared trauma that we helped each other heal from, and a commitment to building something better than what either of us had experienced before.

REFLECTION QUESTIONS:

~ What does it mean to build a relationship on mutual healing rather than just attraction?
~ How important is it to have family support when you're starting a new chapter in life?
~ What role does financial trust and partnership play in a strong marriage?

CHAPTER 24

THE BEST FATHER JOE EVER HAD

BUILDING OUR FOUNDATION

After Richard and I got married, my father and Ida finally allowed Joe to live with us full-time. When Richard came home from work each day, he didn't arrive empty-handed. He always had something for Joe—a pencil, an eraser, a simple ball—small gestures that meant everything.

Joe noticed, and it brought them closer together. Richard was trying to fill that void, trying to prove that Joe mattered. It worked beautifully.

Soon, Joe didn't want to go to my parents' place on weekends anymore. We didn't need fancy meals—just a TV dinner, a bit of creativity, and we had ourselves a satisfying meal. We'd go to the corner store for treats, one flavor one day, another the next. These simple pleasures created bonds that truly mattered.

You don't need expensive things to show someone you care. It's about time, concern, and being present. That's what we learned and embraced. We shared meals, laughter, and moments that money can't buy.

Richard, being from the military, sat Joe down one day and established clear expectations. "You've got to call me Dad or Pops, and your mom is Mom or Mommy—no more calling her Nell. She's not your sister anymore."

Joe paid attention because when he didn't follow these rules, Richard would pull out his belt and wave it in the air. Every time Joe would slip and call me "Nell" or "Baby Nell," he'd look at Richard and correct himself immediately.

Joe had more respect for Richard because he called him Dad. He wanted a father figure and needed one since his biological father had passed away without us even knowing.

I was happy about their relationship, but deep down, I felt insecure. I felt like I was losing my son to the greatest man on earth, my husband Richard. It stemmed from my response to my stepmother marrying my father—initially, I had been jealous of her too.

My stepmother Ida told me it was natural to feel that way. She said it was the same feeling I was having about Joe choosing Richard, and it was okay to feel that way. She encouraged me to talk about it with Richard and let him know what was going on.

Richard took over Joe's life, making him his project. And I'll give credit where it's due—he did everything perfectly with Joe. The way they connected was like puzzle pieces fitting together, and slowly, my insecurity started to fade away.

Feeling insecure is okay and normal. When I recognized it in myself, I acknowledged it and brought it to the attention of those involved. That's how I dealt with it constructively.

Richard wanted Joe to go to school in our neighborhood, but there was nobody to pick him up after school except Mrs. Alfred. When we moved to 501 Hendrix Street, Richard found someone to pick Joe up and bring him safely home.

REFLECTION QUESTIONS:

- How do you handle feelings of insecurity when someone you love forms a strong bond with another person?
- What does it mean to put a child's needs above your own emotional comfort?
- How can step-parents build relationships with children while respecting the biological parent's role?

CHAPTER 25

CREATING OUR HOME

501 HENDRIX STREET

When Joe was nine years old, my life was hit with devastating trauma. It all started the night I watched my best friend take her last breath. She was the wife of Richard's brother Nathaniel and the mother of five beautiful children.

I don't want to get into all the details of how I ended up in that hospital that night, pregnant with Ricky and not even knowing it. I couldn't remember what happened for such a long time. The painful memories of that evening kept me in and out of the hospital for most of my pregnancy with Ricky.

Her beautiful face kept haunting me, and the pain of losing her was too much to bear. But I wasn't the only one who suffered—her husband lost the love of his life, and her children lost their mother.

Those five devastated children came into my life like a whirlwind. It was like a storm hitting me, leaving me shattered, feeling like I wanted to disappear. My husband worked tirelessly, holding us all together while we tried to make sense of it all.

The five children stayed with us in our house after their mother passed. My brother-in-law Nathaniel couldn't manage looking after them daily as they reminded him of his deceased wife, though he always provided for them financially.

Living at 501 Hendrix Street with five additional children, the kids all squeezed into our big living room. Joe joined them by sleeping on the floor—all of them still young, with only one not yet school-aged.

I was drowning in despair, wishing for an escape from this overwhelming weight. Joe loved his cousins, and they were together like brothers and sisters. We didn't separate them because they truly loved each other. When Ricky was born, he completed our family and brought new joy amidst the chaos.

When we had to face court about the children's custody, just the adults went. They wanted to give everyone a chance at caring for them. I told the judge everything, baring my soul, and pleaded that I couldn't bear to see those kids separated. I'd rather die than see them torn apart.

I cried so hard, and the judge—this little Jewish man—felt it and understood. He granted me custody of those five children without papers or signatures, just my word and agreement from everyone involved.

We were living on the first floor with a big pallet on the living room floor. It was like a sleepover every day. When I told our landlord, the Ginsburgs, our story, Mr. Ginsburg said we could fix up the basement.

We transformed that basement at 501 Hendrix Street into a haven. Joe was thrilled to have his cousins with him. We painted and turned that space into their sanctuary—the boys had their own rules down there with several rooms to choose from.

The landlord had friends who owned furniture stores nearby. His friend wanted to help and provided beds for the children so they wouldn't have to sleep on the floor anymore. Another friend sold sheets and blankets and gave us free supplies.

If you share your story and express your needs, people will reach out to help. Even the PathMark grocery store used to give people in the neighborhood leftover fruit and vegetables before they spoiled. People can be incredibly good.

REFLECTION QUESTIONS:

- How do you find strength to care for others when you're dealing with your own trauma?
- What does it mean to open your heart and home to children in need?
- How have you seen community support emerge during times of crisis?

CHAPTER 26

ADVENTURES AND CHALLENGES

ON THE ROAD AGAIN

Every summer, all of us would pile into the car for our adventures, visiting family and creating memories. Life seemed good on the surface, but deep down, I was still shattered in ways I couldn't articulate.

It wasn't long before I found myself pregnant again with Reba. Just like that, it was time for the same trip down to South Carolina with those five children during the summer.

When I look back now, it was wonderful—like a whole life of vitamins that puts a smile on someone's face and spreads happiness all around. On our way back with those pizza-filled kids in the car, it felt like nothing could bring us down.

Richard's sister entered the picture with her two children, adding to our traveling group. Every time we stopped for bathroom breaks, people would look at us like we were crazy. "You've got all those children in the car?" they'd say.

But the children didn't care as long as they felt loved. We piled them in—my brother-in-law's five children, my sister-in-law's two children, and my three children. The big children sat on the seats while the small ones sat on the floor, and they never complained. They were tough and resilient.

We'd drop off my brother-in-law's five children at their grandmother's house in Sumter, South Carolina, then my sister-in-law's two children in

Hampton, South Carolina. After all that, only Richard, our three children, and I would continue to see Richard's father and his wife.

We even made it to Disney World. My husband always found a way to have money to take us everywhere—boat rides, amusement parks, you name it. We just wanted to enjoy life, and those children had the best time of their lives.

Miss Maggie, the five children's grandmother, eventually said it wasn't fair for us to be packing all those kids in the car like that. She was right—they were growing, and it was getting harder to manage them all.

Thankfully, Miss Maggie was able to care for her grandchildren, so my husband and I made the difficult decision to leave them there. We packed up all their belongings and headed out.

Miss Maggie also pointed out that my sister-in-law had been using us, sending her kids down with us and overcrowding the car. I never said no because I wanted her to accept me. Truth be told, I've always needed acceptance because of my history with rejection.

Sometimes it takes someone outside of you to show you the truth about yourself, and we must be mature enough to receive it. Be true to yourself, even if it hurts someone else. The most important person you can be truthful with is yourself.

It worked out in the end. The children started school in South Carolina, so we didn't have to bring them back to New York anymore. But I was exhausted, running on fumes, with so many loose ends to tie up within myself.

What kept me going? Prayer and my imaginary friend Jesus. I talked to him constantly, unaware that he wasn't imaginary at all. Prayer saved me and got me through those dark, confusing times.

REFLECTION QUESTIONS:

- How do you balance caring for extended family with your own family's needs?
- What does it mean to be used by others, and how do you recognize when it's happening?
- How does faith sustain you during overwhelming periods of your life?

CHAPTER 27

BUILDING WEALTH WITH PURPOSE

REAL ESTATE INVESTING

Sometimes in life, we miss opportunities because we fail to recognize our true callings. In the fall of 1968, we managed to purchase the house across the street on 492 Hendrix Street by diving into different ventures. I sold wigs, repaired zippers at a local cleaners, sold Tupperware, decorated storefronts, and babysat children.

Each of these smaller businesses contributed to my overall income. I learned how to fix zippers from my older sibling, and I used that skill to make money. My father had passed down the gift of being handy, showing me that you don't need fancy degrees to succeed if you use the talents God has given you.

When we got audited, being uneducated actually helped me. I had written all my financial information on sheets of paper that I kept in a book. I also wrote transaction amounts on the outside of envelopes that contained the money to balance my books.

When the IRS called us to settle, I showed them my makeshift records, and they were so impressed that they closed the case without charging us anything. My accountant used to mock me for writing everything down, but when a flood destroyed her basement and all her clients' records, I had the last laugh.

Degrees and qualifications may hold value, but they mean nothing if you don't pay attention to the gifts that God has given you. God gives us these gifts, not degrees. It's your duty to utilize those gifts, not chase after diplomas.

After purchasing the property on 492 Hendrix Street, I decided to rent out apartments to my girlfriends. I gave each of them an apartment, and as long as they didn't create additional expenses, the rent would never change.

My Jewish friend Betty told me I needed to move into a better environment, and she was right. There comes a time in life when you need to move on, and it's important to bring your friends along if they're willing.

Jean and her three children stayed with us for a year, and I used the rent money to come up with a lump sum of $5,000 to purchase another property. Manufacturers Hanover Trust loaned us $2,000, and I paid the rest with rent money.

Eventually, I was able to purchase three houses on a single block, but it took time to pay off the mortgages. By the time we were both thirty, my husband and I had bought our fifth house at 73 Hill Street in Cypress Hills.

One day, a neighbor expressed disbelief that we could own five houses at such a young age, making negative assumptions. Instead of getting upset, I took the opportunity to explain how we achieved success through hard work, consistency, and good financial management.

We never had to sleep on the streets, but many in our community don't know what to do with money, so they end up spending aimlessly. When I hear about people owning five cars, I wonder why. There are only seven days in a week—why not invest wisely instead?

REFLECTION QUESTIONS:

- How do you identify and develop the natural talents God has given you?
- What does it mean to build wealth for purpose rather than just accumulation?
- How do you stay grounded and generous when you achieve financial success?

CHAPTER 28

SUCCESS WITH MEANING

MILLIONAIRE BY 30

By 1972, we had money because of our property investments, so I got involved with a skincare company called Nu Skin. I became a distributor and decided what I wanted, then went after it.

Not long after joining the company, I was speaking at prestigious hotels in New York City like the Amazon, Holiday Inn, and Marriott. My dear friend Winnie Mae, who is still a millionaire today, became my partner. We had our own office and eventually joined forces with John and Pat Dwyer, brothers who owned seven successful restaurants.

I was the speaker because I wasn't shy about public speaking. Doctors, lawyers, and people from all walks of life would come to hear me speak. It was amazing to have their trust and support.

Chanly and Winnie Ma owned a million-dollar business and introduced me to multi-level marketing through Nu Skin. I knew that if I didn't have a strong financial net worth, they never would have accepted me. Rich people typically don't accept poor people into their circle.

Once they found out about our network and net worth, they welcomed us with open arms. We called ourselves the "Rat Pack," and we lived a life of luxury and style.

But you know what? I thank God because on our way up the ladder, I never forgot my friends from the old days—my Brooklyn friends, my "struggle" friends. Each of my four friends had an apartment in our five houses. I made them caretakers who looked after our other tenants.

I always told them that as long as they helped me maintain the houses and take care of the tenants, they would always have a place to stay, and I would never increase their rent. That's how it played out for all those years.

As our net worth grew into the millions, we didn't let it go to our heads. We enjoyed vacations and had a good life, but we also had Jean and her three boys living with us. Jean's sacrifice and dedication to our household cannot be measured.

Even at our highest point, we never forgot the importance of being practical. Money doesn't define a person. It's not just about becoming a millionaire—it's about having the wisdom and financial knowledge to ensure a secure future.

Moving forward, I drove the same old white car we bought when we had nothing. Even with a net worth of five, six, or seven million dollars, I didn't get excited over finances. You need money to supply your life, but it doesn't define who you are.

My husband's health started failing, and he suggested we sell our properties before it was too late. We were blessed to be millionaires, but we didn't want money to define us.

The purpose of gaining wealth was to elevate my self-esteem, to prove to myself that I am somebody. It wasn't about making money—I never did it for the money. That's a lesson I constantly reminded my children of: never get too attached to money, never think money is everything.

When you prioritize money above all else, you become sad, evil, and unhappy. You end up taking your frustrations out on the world, and that's why people are so angry.

REFLECTION QUESTIONS:

- ∼ How do you define success beyond just financial achievement?
- ∼ What does it mean to lift others up as you climb the ladder of success?
- ∼ How do you maintain your values and relationships when you achieve wealth?

CHAPTER 29

FINDING MY MISSION

THE QUEEN OF QUEENS

By August 1973, we had officially moved to Queens at 147th Avenue. Jean, with her three boys, found herself with no place to stay after coming from North Carolina. Our children went to school together, and that's how we crossed paths.

Jean came to live with us first and even contributed rent money that helped me secure the house on 147th Avenue in Queens. Her contribution that year was crucial in helping us get that property.

During my teenage years as a mother's helper with the LaGrange family, I had learned how to become an expert at cleaning. When we moved in, all the Jewish families moved out, but we didn't keep the front as clean as they had. So I took charge, organized the community, and led by example.

I started cleaning the area around the front of my part of the street and encouraged others to do the same. As the years went by, someone finally took notice of all the organizing and cleaning I was doing.

Betty, who was Jewish and from East New York, had lived in that community for years. She saw the work I put into cleaning and organizing the block, turning chaos into order. She looked at me and said, "Nellie, you need to leave this place and find yourself a better spot."

Betty saw how I rallied the community, getting everyone out early on

Saturday mornings with their hoses, washing down the fronts of their homes. The city used to send a truck to sweep the streets, but when cars were parked on Saturday mornings, that truck couldn't make its rounds.

So I had this idea—we started cleaning porches and working together to keep our street looking fresh and clear. We scrubbed away the dirt and managed to keep it clean at least once a week.

Betty wanted me to step away because she saw a shift happening in the neighborhood. She saw my ambition and encouraged it. Her husband, an attorney, saw something in me too. Betty believed I deserved a better shot, a fresh start.

She knew that if I stayed with the same crowd who had a limited mindset, I was bound to stay stuck there as well. You've got to be strong to break free from that cycle.

Betty took me to Howard Beach to clean her house. When the kids were getting older and I had more freedom, I brought Reba with me. Betty had a little boy Reba's age, and they played together as friends.

Seeing them play together gave me joy, knowing I was doing something my mother wasn't able to do. I was being an example for Reba and others to follow, teaching my children how to manage a household.

Let me lay it out for you—I'm the product of bipolar roots with ADD. Bipolar isn't just some word you throw around; it's the foundation of my so-called "dysfunctional" behavior. But I embrace it because these are gifts passed down through my family tree.

I told my kids that whatever part of this they inherited, they should accept it as a gift. It's the legacy of my mother, who was bipolar and passed it down to me. I tell them not to be embarrassed because I've got ADD and other quirks, and I see them all as gifts from God.

REFLECTION QUESTIONS:

- ~ How do you turn your unique characteristics and challenges into strengths?
- ~ What does it mean to be a positive influence in your community?
- ~ How do you know when it's time to step away from familiar situations to grow?

CHAPTER 30

A HOUSE OF HOPE

BOARDING HOUSE BLESSINGS

My journey of housing and helping those who needed a safe haven began in Queens. It was messy, raw, and confusing, but it was real and the start of something that carved deep into my soul.

I learned a lot during the house parties Richard and I used to host before we got married. Those gatherings taught me about dealing with nightclub operations. Our Friday and Saturday club nights were always bustling with energy. We offered free collard greens, potato salad, and cornbread alongside music and a DJ, charging only for liquor, which allowed us to make good profit.

When folks walked through our door, they knew they didn't need fancy degrees to make it. They just needed to commit and steer themselves in one direction. Every person who came had to strive for higher education—whether a nine-month course, training program, or life lesson.

My husband and I even went back to school at York College to deepen our knowledge in real estate investment. We believed in investing in our children and those who came to us, ensuring they had the best opportunities available.

The finances came from our houses. The profits from those five houses sustained us. I added the nightclub to the mix, and every Friday and Saturday night, that place was thriving.

It wasn't me seeking out broken souls and saying, "Come live with me, I'll fix you up." It was my kids who brought them home. They felt in their hearts that we could help these hurting people.

Reba brought this foster kid from her school who spilled her pain to Reba, who brought it home to me. This girl reached out to us, showing up at our door, haunted by ghosts of her past. In the dead of night, she whispered her truth—a story of unspeakable horrors, of being violated repeatedly by those who were supposed to protect her.

She begged me not to send her back to that foster hell; she'd rather brave the dangers of the streets. Of course, I couldn't turn her away. But in those days, if you didn't report where a lost kid was, you were considered a criminal.

That girl stood strong, defying the officers, saying she'd rather disappear into the night than face another nightmare. And that's what she did—slipped away like a shadow. We searched through rain-soaked streets in our three cars like a pack of wolves hunting for our cub. Against all odds, we found her and held her close.

Nobody, and I mean nobody, was going to have sex or babies in that house. The word had gotten out that I didn't want any promiscuous behavior in my house, and I wasn't going to let that happen on my watch.

It wasn't just about the absence of sex and babies—it was about respect, boundaries, and acknowledging that we're all in this together. Nobody got pregnant in that house, and that wasn't just lucky coincidence. That was the result of hard work, diligence, and making sure everyone understood the consequences.

I knew what everybody was going through. A lot of people didn't know the acts of kindness I extended, even after my own children had grown up and moved away. I opened my doors to those who sought shelter, even people from my church, though nobody in the congregation ever knew.

Why? Because I didn't go spreading their stories as gossip. My tongue was sealed tighter than Fort Knox because I knew that if I talked about what I did, if I betrayed that sacred trust, nobody would trust me anymore.

REFLECTION QUESTIONS:

- How do you create safe spaces for people who have been hurt by those who should have protected them?
- What does it mean to help others without seeking recognition or praise?
- How do you maintain appropriate boundaries while still offering unconditional love?

CHAPTER 31

COMMUNITY AND PURPOSE

WE'RE ALL IN THIS TOGETHER

Looking back at my experiences, including the St. James Hotel, I learned that seniors have a responsibility to guide young people who are being led astray. Even today, I feel this immense responsibility to help young folks make right decisions, to guide them in the right direction, even when they don't understand it at the moment.

It's therapeutic for me to be that guiding figure to others, especially knowing I didn't have that support myself. I've been real with all the girls in my house, telling them the truth. I told them, "Don't let any man use you sexually, because once he gets what he wants, your worth and value are gone to him. He loses respect, plain and simple."

None of my girls in the house got pregnant. Everybody eventually got married and found someone who truly cared, who saw them for more than just a sexual object. That's how it should be. We've got to break this cycle, this belief that all we're good for is giving ourselves up to men's desires.

The teenagers in our house would help prepare food, peeling potatoes and making large quantities of potato salad every Friday and Saturday night. It became a routine that lasted for years, and I have fond memories of those times.

We trusted and spent time with the teenagers, taking them on outings and teaching them valuable life lessons. They learned the importance of giving back, whether contributing a portion of their earnings from outside jobs or paying rent if they wanted to move out.

It wasn't a free ride. Everyone had to roll up their sleeves and pour their soul into keeping our household afloat. We all had our roles and duties laid out clearly—education, running the household, tending to business. Everyone pitched in 10% toward rent.

Someone was in charge of the grocery list, mapping out trips to PathMark in Far Rockaway. We had it all organized like a well-oiled machine, following a program and running that place with precision.

In a way, that place was my first experience running a boarding house. But I called it a home of love because that's what it was. These folks weren't just boarders; they were family.

Take Martha Parker, for instance. She was 103 when she passed away in that house. Everyone rallied around her, taking care of her. The city paid me a small amount monthly for her care, and she gave me her food stamps because she was finally in an environment she wanted and needed.

She had watched her own mother die in a cold nursing home, and we weren't going to let her go through that. She was like a grandmother to my kids, watching them play in the backyard where we had that old swing set.

All these moments unfolded in that house with its six bedrooms—three on the first floor and three in the basement. It was a sanctuary where we fought for a better tomorrow for ourselves and each other.

We never had fights in the house because our mission was real. Everyone saw it and felt it. When you're on a mission, fighting just isn't going to cut it. You've got to stay focused and keep your eyes on the prize.

REFLECTION QUESTIONS:

- What does it mean to create a mission-driven community where everyone has a role?
- How do you teach young people their worth while helping them develop responsibility?
- What legacy do you want to leave through the way you treat and guide others?

CHAPTER 32

WISDOM FOR THE NEXT GENERATION

THE WAY THEY SHOULD GO

When I see people today saying they don't have time to take care of their children, I tell them you've got to organize yourself. You've got to make time for those little ones, for your family. That's what I did with my own daughter, Reba. I learned how to take care of her and teach her right behaviors.

It's important to teach children not just what to do and what not to do, but also why they should or shouldn't do it. For instance, if a child wants to throw a ball inside the house, I wouldn't just say "Don't throw the ball." Instead, I would explain why throwing the ball inside might not be a good idea.

I would say something like, "Don't throw the ball because it might break something or knock things over, and someone could get hurt. It's safer to play with the ball outside or in a different room." This way, the child understands the reason behind my instructions.

By explaining the reasons behind rules, children can better understand the importance of following them. It also helps them develop critical thinking skills and make better decisions in the future. As a parent, it's important to be patient and take time to explain things to children in ways they can understand.

Although I spent a good amount of time doing that, I never allowed my kids to dominate my time. I made sure to take time for myself too, and I still do. I tell my children straight-up, "This time is for me. I need you to go to your room, read a book, or find something else to do." And they respected that because they heard it from me their whole lives.

You've got to learn how to organize your household too. Even when we were struggling financially, we made time for ourselves. We'd walk down the street and grab a lollipop or ice cream cone. It was the little things that kept us going.

You can't be afraid to detach yourself from your children for a little while. They're going to be okay. They'll survive, and they have each other. So you go out there and do what you've got to do, take care of business. When you come back, you'll be renewed and ready to take on whatever comes your way.

There was a specific incident that highlighted the significance of personalized attention. One of the children expressed concern about something they were experiencing. It struck me that these children didn't want or need much money—rather, they desired someone who would listen and take time to understand them.

Some of them lacked guidance and resources because they didn't have anyone to teach or guide them through various aspects of life. In today's world, with easy access to information through the internet, many parents can simply search online for how to teach their kids certain skills. But back then, that wasn't an option for us.

This realization served as another milestone in my journey of understanding how to connect with and guide those around me. It highlighted the importance of being present, actively listening to their concerns, and providing the support and knowledge they lacked.

By nurturing and empowering the minds of folks around me and introducing them to my relationship with Jesus, they too could grow into confident, knowledgeable individuals capable of navigating life's challenges.

The lessons I learned from those two broken sticks—me and Jesus—taught me that being willing to accept the things I couldn't change gave me a superpower. It taught me to be resilient and observant of the actions of others and myself.

God provided people around me to help nurture me during my youth, and I can now see the different roles each person played. Now I could do the same for others—be the person who listens, who guides, who shows up when someone needs help finding their way.

REFLECTION QUESTIONS:

- How do you balance giving time to others while maintaining time for yourself?
- What does it mean to teach children the "why" behind rules and expectations?
- How can you be the kind of person for others that you needed when you were struggling?

A FINAL LETTER TO YOU, DEAR READER

My precious friend,

As you close this book, I want you to know something important: your decision to walk with me through these pages means more than you could ever imagine. You've witnessed my journey from a silent, abandoned child to a woman who learned to break chains and build bridges. But more than that, you've embarked on your own journey of reflection and healing.

If you're reading this and thinking, "My story isn't as dramatic as yours, Nellie," let me stop you right there. Every story of overcoming matters. Every choice to keep going when life gets hard is heroic. Every decision to love when you've been hurt is revolutionary.

Maybe you picked up this book because you're struggling with your own trauma. Maybe someone you love is fighting battles you don't understand. Or maybe you're simply seeking hope in a world that sometimes feels hopeless. Whatever brought you here, I believe it was no accident.

TO THOSE WHO SEE THEMSELVES IN MY STORY:

If you've experienced abandonment, abuse, poverty, or any form of trauma, please know this: your past does not define your future. The silence you may feel trapped in right now is not permanent. The chains that seem unbreakable can be broken. I am living proof of this truth.

Start where you are. Use what you have. Do what you can. And remember—you don't have to do it alone. Whether you find strength in faith, therapy, community, or all of the above, help is available. Hope is real. Healing is possible.

TO THOSE WHO WANT TO HELP OTHERS:

Maybe my story has awakened something in you—a desire to be the person for someone else that you needed in your darkest hour. That calling is sacred and important. The world desperately needs people who will open their hearts and homes to the broken, the lost, the forgotten.

But remember: you can't pour from an empty cup. Take care of your own healing first. Seek support. Build your own foundation of strength. Then, from that solid place, reach out to others.

TO THOSE SEEKING FAITH:

Throughout my story, you've met my "imaginary friend" who turned out to be Jesus. You've seen how faith sustained me through the darkest valleys and greatest triumphs. If you're curious about this relationship, I encourage you to explore it.

But if faith looks different for you, that's okay too. What matters is that you find something greater than yourself to anchor your hope in—whether that's love, service, justice, or the unbreakable human spirit.

TO EVERYONE:

Here's what I want you to remember as you go forward:

- **You are somebody.** Not because of what you've accomplished or how others see you, but simply because you exist. You matter.
- **Your story is important.** Every chapter—the beautiful and the broken—has value. Don't be ashamed of where you've been; use it to help others find their way.

- **Healing is possible.** It may not be quick or easy, but it's real. Don't give up on yourself or your journey.
- **You have more strength than you know.** If you're reading this, you've already survived 100% of your worst days. That's not luck—that's strength.
- **You're not alone.** Even when it feels like you're fighting battles no one understands, you're part of a community of survivors, thrivers, and hope-builders.

As you close this book and return to your own story, carry these truths with you. And remember—the same power that brought me from silence to voice, from abandonment to purpose, from trauma to triumph, is available to you too.

Your story isn't over. In many ways, it's just beginning.

Go build your bridges, dear friend. The world needs what you have to offer.

With all my love and endless hope for your journey,

Nellie Rembert

P.S. If this book has touched your life in any way, please share it with someone who needs hope. Sometimes we become the answered prayer someone has been waiting for.

EPILOGUE

THE BRIDGE OF HEALING

UNDERSTANDING TRAUMA AND FINDING HOPE

Through years of therapy, I have been able to recognize and name my trauma. As you have now come along this journey with me, here is some information I have taken away from counseling and my ever-present friend, Jesus, about how we respond to difficult situations.

Understanding these responses has helped me make sense of my own story and might help you understand yours as well. Whether you call it God, your higher power, or simply the resilience of the human spirit, there is always hope for healing and transformation.

TRAUMA RESPONSE 1: THE "FIGHT" RESPONSE

- **Definition:** Confronting the threat aggressively. This involves reacting to a threat or traumatic event with aggression or confrontation, including verbal arguments or physical fights, driven by a surge of hormones preparing the body for defense.
- **Biblical Example:** Nehemiah rebuilding the walls of Jerusalem

(Nehemiah 4:17–18) "Those who were rebuilding the wall and those who carried burdens carried with one hand doing the work and the other keeping hold of a weapon."
- **The Solution:** Nehemiah combined building with defending, showing reliance on God while staying ready to protect what mattered.

TRAUMA RESPONSE 2: THE "FLIGHT" RESPONSE

- **Definition:** Running away or avoiding the threat. This response involves escaping or avoiding danger, manifesting physically by running away or emotionally through behaviors like giving the silent treatment or refusing to acknowledge problems.
- **Biblical Example:** Hagar fleeing from Sarai (Genesis 16:6–8) "The angel of the Lord found Hagar near a spring in the desert; it was the spring that is beside the road to Shur."
- **The Solution:** An angel of the Lord found Hagar, provided guidance, and assured her of God's plan for her future.

TRAUMA RESPONSE 3: THE "FREEZE" RESPONSE

- **Definition:** Becoming immobile or unable to act in the face of threat. This occurs when the brain is overwhelmed by a traumatic event, leading to paralysis and inability to act, often with decreased heart rate.
- **Biblical Example:** Israelites at the Red Sea (Exodus 14:13–14) "But Moses told the people, 'Don't be afraid. Just stand still and watch the Lord rescue you today.'"
- **The Solution:** Moses reassured the Israelites to trust in God, and God showed Himself faithful by delivering them safely while destroying their enemies.

TRAUMA RESPONSE 4: THE "FAWN" RESPONSE

- **Definition:** Trying to please or placate the threat to avoid conflict. This involves people-pleasing behaviors, such as complying with demands to create temporarily safe environments, though it can perpetuate cycles of abuse.
- **Biblical Example:** Abraham asking Sarah to say she is his sister (Genesis 12:11–13) "Say you are my sister, that it may go well with me because of you, and that my life may be spared for your sake."
- **The Solution:** God protected Sarah and rebuked Pharaoh for taking her. Despite Abraham's fearful actions, Sarah's trust in God was rewarded.

TRAUMA RESPONSE 5: THE "ATTACH" RESPONSE

- **Definition:** Forming attachments to others as a way of finding safety and stability. This manifests as seeking close relationships, relying on others for security, or fear of abandonment.
- **My Story:** This was often my response—desperately seeking acceptance and family wherever I could find it, sometimes putting myself in dangerous situations because I needed to belong somewhere.
- **The Solution:** Learning that our ultimate security comes not from human relationships alone, but from our connection to something greater than ourselves—whether you call it God, the universe, or the unbreakable human spirit.

FINDING YOUR OWN BRIDGE TO HEALING

My journey from a silent, traumatized child to a woman who could build bridges and break chains wasn't easy, but it was possible. Here's what I've learned:

- **Name Your Pain:** You can't heal what you won't acknowledge. It took me decades to understand that my responses were normal reactions to abnormal circumstances.
- **Find Your Support System:** Whether it's therapy, faith, friends, or all of the above, you don't have to heal alone. My imaginary friend Jesus was real all along, providing the relationship that sustained me.
- **Use Your Pain for Purpose:** The very things that wounded me most deeply became the foundation for helping others. Your struggles aren't meaningless—they're preparation for your calling.
- **Build Bridges, Don't Just Break Chains:** It's not enough to escape your past; you have to build something better for yourself and others. Create the family, community, and support you wish you'd had.
- **Maintain Hope:** Even in the darkest moments, even when you can't see the way forward, keep believing that your story isn't over. The same power that brought me from silence to voice, from abandonment to purpose, is available to you too.

Whether you're reading this as someone who shares faith in Jesus or as someone seeking hope from another source, know this: you were created with purpose, you have inherent worth, and your story—no matter how broken it seems—can become a bridge of healing for others.

The chains that once bound me became the very tools I used to help others find freedom. Your pain can become your purpose. Your trauma can transform into triumph. Your broken places can become the places where light gets in.

This is my prayer for you: May you find the courage to name your pain, the strength to seek help, the wisdom to use your experience for good, and the hope to believe that your best days are still ahead of you.

Remember, dear friend: You are somebody. You matter. Your story matters. And you have more strength inside you than you know.

With love and hope for your journey,
Nellie

READER REFLECTION GUIDE

This guide is designed to help you process the themes and lessons from this memoir, whether you're reading alone, with a book club, or as part of a support group.

CHAPTER-BY-CHAPTER REFLECTION QUESTIONS

Chapters 1–5: Early Trauma and Silence

- How do you cope when words fail you or when you feel unheard?
- What role has silence played in your life—as protection, punishment, or preparation?
- Who or what has served as your "imaginary friend" during difficult times?

Chapters 6–10: Family and Identity

- How have family secrets or missing information affected your sense of identity?
- What does "family" mean to you beyond biological relationships?
- Who has served as a father/mother figure when your biological parents couldn't fulfill that role?

Chapters 11–15: Growing Up Too Fast

- How do you take responsibility for your choices while acknowledging vulnerability?
- What generational patterns have you had to break in your own life?
- How have you experienced or witnessed prejudice, and how did you respond?

Chapters 16–20: Finding Independence

- When have you had to rely on the kindness of strangers?
- How do you maintain hope when options are limited?
- What does it mean to build something from nothing?

Chapters 21–25: Building Relationships and Family

- How do you form healthy relationships after experiencing trauma?
- What does it mean to choose family rather than just inherit it?
- How do you handle insecurity in relationships?

Chapters 26–30: Success and Service

- How do you define success beyond financial achievement?
- What does it mean to lift others as you climb?
- How do you use your resources to serve others?

Chapters 31–32: Legacy and Wisdom

- What wisdom do you want to pass on to the next generation?
- How do you balance serving others while maintaining healthy boundaries?
- What legacy do you want to leave?

TRAUMA AND HEALING DISCUSSION QUESTIONS

- **Identifying Your Trauma Responses:** Which of the five trauma responses (Fight, Flight, Freeze, Fawn, Attach) do you recognize in yourself? How have these responses both protected and limited you?
- **Faith and Spirituality:** How do you understand the role of faith, hope, or spiritual connection in healing? Whether or not you share the author's specific faith, what sustains you during difficult times?
- **Breaking Generational Cycles:** What patterns from your family of origin have you had to consciously break? How do you create new, healthier patterns?
- **Community and Support:** How do you create chosen family and support systems? What does healthy community look like to you?
- **Purpose from Pain:** How might your struggles be preparing you to help others? What unique perspective do your experiences give you?

ACTION STEPS FOR PERSONAL GROWTH

WEEK 1-2: SELF-ASSESSMENT

- Journal about your own story, identifying patterns and trauma responses
- Consider what "chains" you need to break and what "bridges" you want to build

WEEK 3-4: SEEKING SUPPORT

- Identify trusted people in your life you can talk to about your struggles
- Research therapy, support groups, or spiritual communities if needed

WEEK 5-6: FINDING PURPOSE

- Consider how your experiences might help others
- Look for volunteer opportunities or ways to serve your community

WEEK 7-8: BUILDING BRIDGES

- Take concrete steps to create the support systems you wish you'd had
- Reach out to someone who might need encouragement

FOR BOOK CLUBS AND GROUP DISCUSSIONS

OPENING QUESTIONS:

- What drew you to this book?
- What aspects of the author's story resonated most with you?

THEMES TO EXPLORE:

- The difference between surviving and thriving
- The role of chosen family vs. biological family
- How trauma can become purpose
- The importance of community in healing
- Breaking cycles of dysfunction

CLOSING QUESTIONS:

- What will you take away from this book?
- How has this story changed your perspective on trauma, healing, or resilience?
- What action will you take as a result of reading this story?

RESOURCES FOR FURTHER HELP

CRISIS SUPPORT:

- **National Suicide Prevention Lifeline:** 988
- **Crisis Text Line:** Text HOME to 741741

TRAUMA AND THERAPY RESOURCES:

- Psychology Today therapist finder
- EMDR International Association
- National Child Traumatic Stress Network

FAITH-BASED SUPPORT:

- Local churches, synagogues, mosques, or spiritual communities
- Christian counseling organizations
- Celebrate Recovery groups

REMEMBER:

Healing is a journey, not a destination. Be patient with yourself as you process this story and your own experiences. You deserve support, love, and the chance to transform your pain into purpose.

COMPREHENSIVE READER REFLECTION AND STUDY GUIDE

HOW TO USE THIS GUIDE

This reflection guide can be used in multiple ways:
- **Personal Study:** Work through at your own pace for self-reflection and growth
- **Book Clubs:** Discussion questions and activities for group conversations
- **Support Groups:** Trauma-informed questions for healing communities
- **Therapeutic Settings:** Resources for counselors and therapists
- **Educational Use:** Classroom discussions about resilience, trauma, and social justice

SECTION 1: PERSONAL REFLECTION JOURNEY

WEEK 1: UNDERSTANDING YOUR STORY

Daily Reflections:

- **Day 1:** Write about your earliest memory. What emotions does it bring up?
- **Day 2:** Who were the "imaginary friends" or sources of comfort in your childhood?
- **Day 3:** What "chains" from your past still affect you today?
- **Day 4:** What "bridges" do you want to build in your life?
- **Day 5:** Who has been a "Mrs. LaGrange" or positive influence in your life?
- **Day 6:** What does "family" mean to you beyond biology?
- **Day 7:** Write a letter to your younger self

Week 1 Processing Questions:

1. What patterns do you notice in your early relationships and attachments?
2. How has trauma or difficult experiences shaped your worldview?
3. What survival strategies did you develop as a child that may no longer serve you?

WEEK 2: IDENTIFYING TRAUMA RESPONSES

Daily Reflections:

- **Day 1:** When do you tend to "fight" (become aggressive or confrontational)?
- **Day 2:** When do you "flee" (avoid, withdraw, or run away)?
- **Day 3:** When do you "freeze" (become paralyzed or unable to act)?
- **Day 4:** When do you "fawn" (people-please or try to placate others)?
- **Day 5:** When do you "attach" (desperately seek connection or fear abandonment)?
- **Day 6:** Which response is most common for you and why?
- **Day 7:** How might understanding these responses help you heal?

WEEK 2 PROCESSING QUESTIONS:

1. How have your trauma responses both protected and limited you?
2. What triggers these responses in your current life?
3. What healthy coping strategies could you develop to replace unhealthy patterns?

WEEK 3: EXPLORING FAITH AND SPIRITUALITY

Daily Reflections:

- **Day 1:** What role has faith, spirituality, or higher power played in your life?
- **Day 2:** What sustains you during your darkest moments?
- **Day 3:** How do you find meaning and purpose in suffering?
- **Day 4:** What does forgiveness mean to you?
- **Day 5:** How do you experience hope, even when circumstances are difficult?
- **Day 6:** What spiritual practices bring you peace?

- **Day 7:** How has your relationship with the divine (however you understand it) evolved?

Week 3 Processing Questions:

1. How do you understand the relationship between faith and healing?
2. What spiritual resources do you need to explore or develop?
3. How can you maintain hope without denying reality?

WEEK 4: BUILDING COMMUNITY AND SUPPORT

Daily Reflections:

- **Day 1:** Who are the people in your life you can truly trust?
- **Day 2:** What does healthy community look like to you?
- **Day 3:** How do you contribute to others' healing and growth?
- **Day 4:** What boundaries do you need to set in relationships?
- **Day 5:** Who might need the support you wish you'd had?
- **Day 6:** How do you ask for help when you need it?
- **Day 7:** What kind of legacy do you want to leave?

Week 4 Processing Questions:

1. How can you build or strengthen your support system?
2. What gifts from your struggle can you offer to others?
3. How do you balance self-care with service to others?

SECTION 2:
BOOK CLUB AND GROUP DISCUSSION GUIDE

MEETING 1: GETTING STARTED (CHAPTERS 1-8)

Opening Question: What drew you to this book, and what are you hoping to get from our discussions?

Key Themes to Discuss:

- The impact of early childhood trauma
- The role of "imaginary friends" or coping mechanisms
- Family separation and its long-term effects
- Finding identity when your origins are unclear

Discussion Questions:

1. How did Nellie's silence at age 9 function as both symptom and protection?
2. What do you think about her relationship with her "imaginary friend"? How do you understand this spiritually and psychologically?
3. How did family separation affect each sibling differently, and what does this teach us about trauma?
4. What role did race and socioeconomic status play in the family's struggles?

Activity: Share (if comfortable) about a person, place, or thing that brought you comfort during a difficult childhood period.

MEETING 2: SURVIVAL AND ADAPTATION (CHAPTERS 9-16)

Opening Question: How do you define resilience, and what does it look like in Nellie's story?

Key Themes to Discuss:

- Premature responsibility and growing up too fast
- The vulnerability of young women seeking love and attention
- Survival strategies that may be both helpful and harmful
- The kindness of strangers vs. predatory behavior

Discussion Questions:

1. How do you balance taking responsibility for choices while acknowledging vulnerability and exploitation?
2. What do you think about Nellie's experience with Joe's father? How do we discuss teenage sexuality and consent?
3. How did strangers like the bus conductor and train conductor serve as "angels" in her story?
4. What does Nellie's experience teach us about poverty, resourcefulness, and dignity?

Activity: Discuss a time when a stranger showed you unexpected kindness or when you showed kindness to someone in need.

MEETING 3: BUILDING RELATIONSHIPS AND FAMILY (CHAPTERS 17-24)

Opening Question: What does "chosen family" mean to you?

Key Themes to Discuss:

- Learning to trust and love after trauma
- Creating family structures that work
- The role of male figures in healing father wounds
- Building relationships across racial and cultural lines

Discussion Questions:

1. How did Bob serve as both helper and potential complication in Nellie's life?
2. What did you think about her relationship with Richard and how they built their marriage?
3. How did Richard become a father to Joe, and what does this teach us about step-parenting?
4. What role did therapy and counseling play in Nellie's ability to form healthy relationships?

Activity: Share about someone who became "family" to you even though you weren't related.

MEETING 4: SUCCESS AND SERVICE (CHAPTERS 25-32)

Opening Question: How do you define success, and how has that definition changed over time?

Key Themes to Discuss:

- Building wealth with purpose
- Using success to help others

- Creating community and safe spaces
- Transforming pain into purpose

Discussion Questions:

1. What do you think about Nellie's approach to real estate investing and building wealth?
2. How did she balance financial success with maintaining her values and relationships?
3. What was the significance of the boarding house and helping vulnerable young people?
4. How did she break generational cycles while honoring her past?

Activity: Discuss how you might use your own experiences, skills, or resources to help others.

MEETING 5: HEALING AND LEGACY (EPILOGUE AND REFLECTION)

Opening Question: What will you take away from Nellie's story?

Key Themes to Discuss:

- Understanding trauma responses
- The role of faith in healing
- Building bridges for the next generation
- Creating lasting change

Discussion Questions:

1. Which of the five trauma responses do you most identify with, and why?
2. How do you understand the role of faith or spirituality in Nellie's healing?
3. What does it mean to transform trauma into triumph?

4. How can we create communities where people like young Nellie would be protected and nurtured?

Closing Activity: Each person shares one action they'll take as a result of reading this book and participating in these discussions.

SECTION 3:
THERAPEUTIC AND SUPPORT GROUP APPLICATIONS

FOR MENTAL HEALTH PROFESSIONALS

Using This Book in Therapy:

- ∼ Bibliotherapy for trauma survivors
- ∼ Exploring resilience and post-traumatic growth
- ∼ Understanding cultural and historical trauma contexts
- ∼ Family therapy discussions about generational patterns

Key Therapeutic Themes:

- ∼ Attachment trauma and its effects
- ∼ Developing healthy coping mechanisms
- ∼ Building secure relationships after betrayal
- ∼ Finding meaning and purpose through suffering

Cautions and Considerations:

- ∼ May be triggering for survivors of childhood abuse
- ∼ Discuss racial trauma and its ongoing effects
- ∼ Address economic factors in trauma and recovery
- ∼ Consider faith/spirituality issues for diverse clients

FOR SUPPORT GROUPS

Trauma Survivor Groups:

- ∼ Use reflection questions to explore personal healing journeys
- ∼ Discuss trauma responses without shame or judgment
- ∼ Explore healthy vs. unhealthy coping mechanisms
- ∼ Build community and mutual support

Parenting Groups:

- ∼ Discuss breaking generational cycles
- ∼ Explore healthy discipline and boundary-setting
- ∼ Address the impact of parental trauma on children
- ∼ Build skills for creating safe, nurturing homes

Faith-Based Groups:

- ∼ Explore the role of faith in healing
- ∼ Discuss biblical responses to trauma
- ∼ Address questions about suffering and God's presence
- ∼ Build spiritual practices that support healing

SECTION 4: EDUCATIONAL APPLICATIONS

FOR HIGH SCHOOL AND COLLEGE CLASSROOMS

American History/Social Studies:

- ∼ Discuss the Great Migration and its effects on families
- ∼ Explore segregation's impact on individuals and communities
- ∼ Examine economic inequality and its generational effects
- ∼ Analyze the civil rights era from a personal perspective

Psychology/Social Work:

- ∼ Study trauma responses and resilience factors
- ∼ Explore attachment theory and its applications
- ∼ Discuss the role of community in mental health
- ∼ Examine cultural factors in healing and recovery

Literature/Writing:

- ∼ Analyze memoir as a literary form
- ∼ Explore voice, authenticity, and storytelling
- ∼ Discuss the ethics of telling traumatic stories
- ∼ Practice reflective and therapeutic writing

Ethics/Philosophy:
- ⁓ Explore questions of forgiveness and justice
- ⁓ Discuss individual vs. societal responsibility
- ⁓ Examine the role of faith in human suffering
- ⁓ Consider what we owe to vulnerable members of society

SECTION 5:
ACTION STEPS AND RESOURCES

30-DAY CHALLENGE: BREAKING CHAINS AND BUILDING BRIDGES

Week 1: Self-Assessment

- **Day 1-2:** Complete trauma response assessment
- **Day 3-4:** Identify personal "chains" to break
- **Day 5-7:** Envision "bridges" you want to build

Week 2: Seeking Support

- **Day 8-10:** Research therapy or counseling options
- **Day 11-12:** Connect with supportive friends or family
- **Day 13-14:** Explore spiritual/faith communities if interested

Week 3: Skill Building

- **Day 15-17:** Practice new coping strategies
- **Day 18-19:** Set healthy boundaries in relationships
- **Day 20-21:** Develop self-care routines

Week 4: Service and Legacy

- **Day 22-24:** Identify ways to help others
- **Day 25-26:** Take concrete action to serve your community

- **Day 27–28:** Share your story (when ready and appropriate)
- **Day 29–30:** Plan for continued growth and healing

RESOURCES FOR CONTINUED HEALING

Crisis and Emergency Support:

- **National Suicide Prevention Lifeline:** 988
- **Crisis Text Line:** Text HOME to 741741
- **National Child Abuse Hotline:** 1-800-4-A-CHILD (1-800-422-4453)
- **National Domestic Violence Hotline:** 1-800-799-7233

Mental Health Resources:

- **Psychology Today Therapist Finder:** psychologytoday.com
- **SAMHSA National Helpline:** 1-800-662-4357
- **National Alliance on Mental Illness:** nami.org
- **Trauma Recovery Network:** traumarecoverynetwork.org

Specialized Trauma Therapy:

- **EMDR International Association:** emdria.org
- **International Society for Traumatic Stress Studies:** istss.org
- **National Child Traumatic Stress Network:** nctsn.org
- **Body-based trauma therapy resources:** sensorimotor.org

Faith-Based Support:

- **American Association of Christian Counselors:** aacc.net
- **Jewish Family Services (various locations)**
- **Islamic counseling resources through local mosques**
- **Celebrate Recovery:** celebraterecovery.com

Books for Continued Reading:

- "The Body Keeps the Score" by Bessel van der Kolk
- "Trauma and Recovery" by Judith Herman
- "Rising Strong" by Brené Brown
- "Option B" by Sheryl Sandberg and Adam Grant
- "The Gifts of Imperfection" by Brené Brown

Support Groups:

- **Adult Children of Alcoholics:** adultchildren.org
- **Survivors of Incest Anonymous:** siawso.org
- **Co-Dependents Anonymous:** coda.org
- **Al-Anon Family Groups:** al-anon.org

CREATING YOUR OWN SUPPORT NETWORK

Step 1: Assess Your Current Support

- List the people you can talk to about difficult topics
- Identify professionals who support your mental health
- Note spiritual or faith communities you're part of
- Recognize gaps in your support system

Step 2: Build Professional Support

- Research therapists who specialize in trauma
- Consider group therapy or support groups
- Explore spiritual direction or pastoral counseling
- Look into trauma-informed medical care

Step 3: Strengthen Personal Relationships

- Nurture existing healthy relationships
- Set boundaries with toxic or unhealthy people

- Practice vulnerability with safe people
- Build reciprocal support relationships

Step 4: Give Back

- Volunteer with organizations that help trauma survivors
- Mentor someone who's walking a path you've traveled
- Share your story when appropriate and helpful
- Advocate for policies that protect vulnerable people

SECTION 6:
REFLECTION PROMPTS FOR JOURNALING

WEEKLY JOURNALING PROMPTS

Week 1: Your Origin Story

- What messages did you receive about your worth as a child?
- Who were the adults who made you feel safe or unsafe?
- What dreams did you have that were encouraged or discouraged?
- How has your understanding of your childhood changed over time?

Week 2: Survival Strategies

- What did you do to cope with difficult situations as a child?
- Which of these strategies still serve you today?
- Which strategies now limit or harm you?
- What new skills do you want to develop?

Week 3: Relationships and Trust

- How do you decide who to trust?
- What patterns do you notice in your relationships?
- Where do you struggle with boundaries?
- How do you show and receive love?

Week 4: Purpose and Legacy
- How has your pain contributed to your purpose?
- What do you want to be remembered for?
- How do you want to impact others' lives?
- What would you tell your younger self?

DAILY REFLECTION QUESTIONS

- What am I grateful for today?
- What challenged me, and how did I respond?
- Where did I see growth or healing in my life?
- How did I connect with others or with something greater than myself?
- What do I need to release or forgive today?

REMEMBER:

Healing is not a destination but a journey. Be patient with yourself, seek support when you need it, and celebrate every step forward, no matter how small.

www.ingramcontent.com/pod-product-compliance
Lightning Source LLC
Chambersburg PA
CBHW070511090426
42735CB00012B/2736

A JOURNEY OF TRAUMA, FAITH, AND FREEDOM

BREAKING CHAINS
AND
BUILDING BRIDGES

NELLIE REMBERT

Copyright © 2025 by Dr. Reba Perry-Ufele
Published by Building Wealth Four Generations INC d/b/a
The 1 and Only
All rights reserved.

No part of this book may be reproduced, transmitted, or used in any form or by any means—electronic, mechanical, photocopying, recording, or otherwise—without prior written permission from the publisher, except in the case of brief quotations used in critical reviews or articles.

Scripture quotations are taken from the Holy Bible, New International Version® (NIV®). Copyright ©1973, 1978, 1984, 2011 by Biblica, Inc.™ Used by permission. All rights reserved worldwide.

ISBN: 979-8-89741-012-5
EBOOK ISBN: 979-8-89741-013-2

Contributors:
Editor: Kealia Hamilton
Editor: Jori O'Neale

For permission requests, please contact:
The 1 and Only
4500 Forbes Boulevard, STE 200
Lanham, MD 20706
info@the1andonlypublishing.com
www.the1andonlypublishing.com